T0125617

ADDITIONAL PRAISE
FOR *LEAN ON*

"Andreas's groundbreaking book shares a perspective rarely heard and often overlooked. As more and more women lean in to their careers, having someone at home to lean on will become more and more important."

MO FATHELBAB, *keynote speaker and author of* The Friendship Advantage

"Written from his perspective as the supportive husband of a professional spouse, Andreas explores the challenges faced navigating this nontraditional role. More than simply promoting awareness, *Lean On* offers practical solutions for couples working toward mutually fulfilling relationships in a changing society. A truly insightful read."

JENNIFER OWENS, *president, Lakeshore Advantage*

"As the primary breadwinner in our family, Andreas Wilderer's principles that he outlines in his book, *Lean On: The Five Pillars of Support for Women in Leadership,* is a refreshing affirmation of the decisions my husband and I have made to support my career and positive lifestyle for our children and family. Informative and easily understandable, *Lean On* is a must-read for those men and women looking to break the stereotypes of what traditional roles look like and embrace what is right for you."

MELIA TOURANGEAU, *president and CEO, Pittsburgh Symphony Orchestra*

"Unfortunately, it's not until later in life that men and woman understand that life has many phases and the decisions you make along the way have long-lasting impacts on the family. We as a society have believed the career decisions are centered around the male in the family, but that has changed, and I am happy it has changed. I am not happy because of being a female, I am happy because now many men are experiencing the joys of being their children's primary caregivers. They are also experiencing the bias that our society has on many fronts, because they experience the bias that society has on men that have made that decision. I believe this book, *Lean On*, is way overdue and hopefully will make both sexes reflect on how it's not about who is working but about what is best, at a point in time in the journey of life, for their particular 'family unit.' It is our job, when we make the decision to have children, to deliver contributing, self-supporting, and well-grounded human beings to the world."
SHEILA G. TALTON, *CEO and president, Gray Matter Analytics, Inc.*

"Andreas Wilderer's book, *Lean On: The Five Pillars of Support for Women in Leadership,* is a refreshing take on how spouses, partners, and families can bring their skills, talents, and abilities together to complement one another and the family. This is an easy-to-read, principle-based approach on how to create a strong family unit by connecting to the vision of each individual and the needs of the family to create the best that can be, personally and professionally. Bravo for having such an abundance mentality and positive approach to maximizing the whole!"
STEVEN R. SHALLENBERGER, *author of the number-one national bestseller,* Becoming Your Best: The 12 Principles of Highly Successful Leaders; *founder, Becoming Your Best Global Leadership*

"The commitment to strengthen individual and collective leadership in communities has been my professional passion. Personally, I have also been devoted to building capacity in women leaders across a spectrum of professions and career stages. Female leadership has indeed come a long way in the past years, but the structures required to support continued progress in this arena are often overlooked. *Lean On* not only highlights the fundamentals that give rise to the situation but, more importantly, through its Five Pillars framework, provides solutions for individuals, companies, and communities interested in making a positive difference in this arena."
ARADHNA MALHOTRA OLIPHANT, *president and CEO, Leadership Pittsburgh Inc. and president of International Women's Forum of Pittsburgh*

"In my opinion Andreas's book *Lean On* has been long overdue. Like Sheryl Sandberg's *Lean In* it is an absolute eye-opener for those who have never thought about the dramatic changes taking place in partnerships and society. At the same time it is stimulating and encouraging for those who really care about equality."
HEINER THORBORG, *founder of Club Generation CEO and coauthor of* Oben Ohne *(No Women Leaders at the Top)*

"*Lean On* does for stay-at-home dads what Sheryl Sandberg's *Lean In* did for women in the workplace by changing how we think about fathers who choose the nontraditional roles of support-giver, stay-at-home dad, and hearth-keeper. May others follow his lead."
MCKEEL HAGERTY, *CEO of Hagerty*

LEAN ON

ANDREAS WILDERER

LEAN ON

THE FIVE PILLARS
OF SUPPORT FOR WOMEN IN LEADERSHIP

Advantage®

Published by Advantage, Charleston, South Carolina.
Member of Advantage Media Group.

ADVANTAGE is a registered trademark, and the Advantage colophon is a trademark of Advantage Media Group, Inc.

Printed in the United States of America.

10 9 8 7 6 5 4 3 2 1

ISBN: 978-1-64225-082-4
LCCN: 2019912417

Book design by Carly Blake.

This publication is designed to provide accurate and authoritative information in regard to the subject matter covered. It is sold with the understanding that the publisher is not engaged in rendering legal, accounting, or other professional services. If legal advice or other expert assistance is required, the services of a competent professional person should be sought.

 Advantage Media Group is proud to be a part of the Tree Neutral® program. Tree Neutral offsets the number of trees consumed in the production and printing of this book by taking proactive steps such as planting trees in direct proportion to the number of trees used to print books. To learn more about Tree Neutral, please visit **www.treeneutral.com**.

Advantage Media Group is a publisher of business, self-improvement, and professional development books and online learning. We help entrepreneurs, business leaders, and professionals share their Stories, Passion, and Knowledge to help others Learn & Grow. Do you have a manuscript or book idea that you would like us to consider for publishing? Please visit **advantagefamily.com** or call **1.866.775.1696**.

This book is dedicated to all the amazing women who follow their dreams and reach for the stars and to everyone who supports them on their journey.

And to my wonderful wife, Mirka, and our children Dominik and Viktoria, who supported me in writing this book.

CONTENTS

THE FIVE PILLARS

Years ago, as a volunteer firefighter, I learned I must be able to depend on my partner and my partner must be able to depend on me. Unless we worked well together and stayed by each other's side, we would lose the battle. As a team, we could succeed. Together, we were strong.

This is a book about supporting your partner in life and working together as a team. When your partner can depend on you, and when you can depend on your partner, you can beat back the most difficult challenges and build a rewarding future for your entire family. Together, you are strong.

In her 2013 bestseller *Lean In*, Sheryl Sandberg details the challenges that women face in the workplace and urges them to "lean in" to their careers. Her influential book has inspired many women and girls to break free of self-limiting expectations and aspire to become the leaders that they were meant to be.

That does not mean that a woman with an illustrious career cannot also lead a fulfilling family life. Many do, and they often have managed to do both as a one-woman show. Many others, however, express their gratitude for a supportive partner at home who makes it all possible, either one who fairly shares in the responsibilities of the household, or one who manages the household full-time.

In this book, we will take a closer look at how each partner can better support the other, whether in the workplace or in the home. We will see how successful partners have learned to depend on each other. As women leaders *lean in* to their careers, they often have someone to *lean on*—all the better as, together, they reach for their dreams.

Strong support requires a sound structure. Since antiquity, architects have used pillars as fundamental support elements in buildings. Rising from the foundation, load-bearing pillars can be beautiful, functional, and enduring as they support everything from arches and beams to cathedral ceilings.

If a relationship is to be beautiful, functional, and enduring, it, too, must rise from a sound foundation and rest upon powerful pillars that carry the weight together. The master architect of a relationship must not only design them to last but also keep the structure in good condition. If any of the pillars should crumble, the structure will collapse, leaving rubble, not of arches and beams but of dreams.

Through the research for this book, I met so many incredible men and women that are supporting each other in the new normal of gender roles and family models. Despite all their unique oaths and relationships, their similarities stood out in how they build the foundation of their partnerships. I summarize these in five powerful pillars of supportive relationships, which you will find referenced in the pages ahead.

PILLARS OF SUPPORTIVE RELATIONSHIPS

THE PILLAR OF SELF
THE PILLAR OF PARTNERSHIP
THE PILLAR OF FAMILY
THE PILLAR OF THE WORKPLACE
THE PILLAR OF SOCIETY

Because the pillars must work together as a whole, you will not find chapters focused on an individual pillar, but rather, each chapter refers to a selective combination of them. As we examine the architecture of supportive relationships, I will identify at the outset of every chapter the pillars that will be highlighted. However, remember that none can be truly understood out of context with the others.

My wife, Mirka, and I have rallied those pillars through the years to build our own enduring marriage, and we continue to work on it, day by day and year by year. She is a C-suite executive with a demanding career that often takes her far from home on business trips. Her income supports our family. I support her, in turn, by caring for our two children and managing our household.

Mirka's sacrifice has made our family life possible. My sacrifice has made her career possible, but I am doing for her only what women traditionally have done for their husbands for generations. And I am not alone. In today's society, men increasingly are stepping forward to assume that supportive role, though we don't hear much about them. This nontraditional model is just one of a variety of family structures that we will examine, but it is an increasingly common one that plays a critical role as women advance in business leadership.

In following Mirka's career, we left Germany for the United States, moving from Pennsylvania to Colorado to Michigan and back to Pennsylvania. In the early years, as a young family who had just immigrated to a new country, we struggled with our own life, but by the time we arrived in Michigan, we were able to start giving back and become active in the community. Mirka began a mentorship program to encourage young women in leadership, and I began to look into the issue of support for women leaders. Who could help them focus on their careers? Whom could they lean on? I began my research by talking with men about their support role in their partnerships.

As I became involved in the Young Presidents' Organization (YPO), I saw a problem that is common in society: The voices of men who support their wives are not being heard yet. YPO, along with many other organizations that are still trying to catch up with including and supporting women members, had not recognized how many men were stepping up to support these women in their quest for leadership. To help build awareness, I started a male-spouse partner network to give supportive men a platform on which to interact.

I began hearing common themes as I got to know those men. For one thing, they were tired of getting flowers and scarves as gifts when accompanying their wives to functions. "The event planners always seem to presume we're women!" they told me. Though that might seem to be a relatively small matter, it is emblematic of the issues and attitudes that we will examine in these chapters. And, as we will see, change starts in the small places.

In the years since, I have spoken with hundreds of other men around the world who, as I am, are the partners of women with high-powered careers. Some of those men have challenging careers of their own. Others devote themselves full-time to household duties or maintain a flexible part-time job that is compatible with their primary domestic responsibilities. Some have children; others do not. Some have recently retired or sold a business and switched roles with their wives, who have returned to work after years of running the household. My observations from real life experience are very similar to those of Betsy Myers, director of the Center for Women and Business at Bentley University in Waltham, Massachusetts. She categorizes the women in three general family models: late bloomers, half of a power couple, and breadwinners. According to Myers, these categories are described as follows: "the late-bloomers, whose careers hit their stride later in life after they have taken care of children; the one half of a power couple, where both partners are in demanding jobs; and the breadwinners, who often have stay-at-home husbands or spouses who work in flexible jobs."[1]

Listening to what life was like for those men, I realized that my own experiences could prove valuable in assisting others who were adjusting to a new role within their families, or who were anticipating such a shift. I resolved to write a book about the changing nature of leadership in families and workplaces, but it would do more than promote awareness and point out problems; it would offer real solutions. That also was the spirit in which Mirka and I founded our coaching company, Globularity. I already had been advising friends and acquaintances on life skills and business matters, and we envisioned a coaching business that would allow us to extend our reach.

Though the details differ, I have much in common with countless men who are stepping forward to boldly lead their families in a way much different from the way in which their fathers had led theirs. I recognize their story because it is mine, too, and it is one that has largely gone untold. It is time now for those men to step out of the shadows.

---

1   "High-powered Women and Supportive Spouses: Who's in Charge, and of What?" Wharton University of Pennsylvania, accessed June 18, 2019, https://knowledge.wharton.upenn.edu/article/high-powered-women-and-supportive-spouses-whos-in-charge-and-of-what-2/.

THE PILLARS
OF SUPPORT

My logo for the five pillars is the circular design that you see featured on the cover of this book. The circle communicates unity, as all the pillars must work together for optimal strength. Think of that logo as a view of the five architectural pillars from above, each connected by the arches of the superstructure that they support. And now imagine that you are looking, instead, at a circle of people, their arms around one another's shoulders. The logo represents a theme that flows throughout our discussion: Together, we are strong.

Here, then, is a summary of the five pillars. As you turn these pages, you will learn much more. We will see that the strength of each pillar depends on effective communication with your partner, your children, your colleagues, and with the many others who are stepping forward to change our society as you are. And it all starts with your getting to know yourself. To be a supportive partner, you must understand your own strengths.

THE PILLAR OF SELF

Before you can become a supportive partner, you must be self-aware; you must "know thyself," as the ancient Greeks advised. Who are you? How and where do you fit in? We will look at tools such as CliftonStrengths, useful for assessing the qualities that you can bring to any job, any career, any relationship. You will be happiest when you feel authentic in your role, whether in the workplace or in the family. On the other hand, if you are not happy with yourself, feeling that you are out of touch with the real you, how can you expect to contribute meaningfully to anyone else's happiness?

When you and your partner have identified your individual strengths, you will be better able to define the appropriate roles for each of you. If you come to that understanding at the start and establish a timeline, you will be able someday to look back without regrets, even if life takes unexpected turns. You will know that you sacrificed willingly and purposefully. You were not just some victim of circumstance. When you know the real you, you can be confident that you are contributing your unique combination of skills and talents. If you know your dreams and goals, you can feel at peace with the choices that you have made.

WHEN YOU KNOW THE REAL YOU, YOU CAN BE CONFIDENT THAT YOU ARE CONTRIBUTING YOUR UNIQUE COMBINATION OF SKILLS AND TALENTS.

THE PILLAR OF PARTNERSHIP

The traditional model of husband as provider and wife as homemaker still prevails in many families, but it is far from the only one. With about seventy-five million women in the US workforce, the reverse arrangement is being increasingly adopted, and often, each partner shares the responsibility for both providing and homemaking. We will look at those changing models and ways in which couples can adapt to meet their specific needs and circumstances. Every type of partnership has its challenges.

The pillar of partnership is about just the two of them, not their roles as parents if they have children. The partners must follow through on what they are starting and offer meaningful support to each other that is based upon mutual respect. Are they strong

THE PARTNERS MUST FOLLOW THROUGH ON WHAT THEY ARE STARTING AND OFFER MEANINGFUL SUPPORT TO EACH OTHER THAT IS BASED UPON MUTUAL RESPECT.

enough to swim against the current of society's expectations of men and women? If the man earns less than the woman, for example, or if he loses his confidence and sense of identity, will she continue to respect him? Will he respect himself?

Throughout these chapters, we will explore such issues. We will see how partners can work together to set up their household as a well-run business, with a clear purpose and well-defined plans. Each partner also must be sensitive to the other's emotional needs. For example, a woman who devotes her time to a demanding career still wants to feel she is a good mother to her children. She hasn't given up that role. And a man who devotes his time to the daily demands of the household still wants to feel like a provider, which, in a very real way, he is.

THE PILLAR OF FAMILY

If the couple has children, this is the pillar that supports their well-being. In a traditional family structure, the wife takes care of the kids while the husband is at work. In a nontraditional structure, however, the woman still watches out for them. She still cares. Because her career demands much of her time and energy, she wants to know that someone is there. If that is her husband, she must be able to lean on him for that support, and he must follow through on providing it. Meanwhile, if he, too, pursues a career, they must work together to accommodate both their schedules and provide reliable family support, perhaps with the help of third parties.

As Mom and Dad develop a family structure that works for them, a big question remains: Does it work for the children? Kids want to fit in. They don't want their friends to think of them as different, and their friends from traditional families are bound to ask questions such as why their dad is Mr. Mom. Caring parents should make sure their children understand the rationale of their family structure. The kids need reassurance that they are normal, and that they are loved, and that all is well. They need parents who pay attention to their hearts.

Growing up in a nontraditional family can help children gain sensitivity and compassion for other cultures and lifestyles, and it helps them break free of the gender stereotypes that pervade our society. They will not distinguish between "men's work" and "women's duties." They will care only about what works best. Such biases have held back countless people from

IN A NONTRADITIONAL FAMILY, PARENTS HAVE A PRIME OPPORTUNITY TO TEACH THEIR CHILDREN BY EXAMPLE THAT THEY NEED NOT FIT INTO ANYBODY'S MOLD BUT CAN STRIVE TO REACH THEIR FULL POTENTIAL WHATEVER THE MOLD.

reaching their potential. In a nontraditional family, parents have a prime opportunity to teach their children by example that they need not fit into anybody's mold but can strive to reach their full potential whatever the mold.

THE PILLAR OF THE WORKPLACE

As women rise to positions of greater leadership in the workplace, they continue to struggle against the same obstacles that long have sought to hold them down: unequal pay, the glass ceiling, and sexual harassment, to name a few. Increasingly they are speaking out to demand the dignity that they deserve and turning their attention to the next generation, inspiring girls to aspire to greatness. A supportive workplace is essential because anything that threatens to hold back the woman's career is also a threat to the well-being of the partnership and family. Nonetheless, the workplace has remained a daunting environment for many.

Not only do women face attitudes in the workplace that threaten to hold them back but society also can be unkind to men who choose to postpone their careers to manage their household. It takes a real man with a lot of self-confidence to handle this. Women executives often hear the question, so what does your husband do? He can't just be sitting at home all day! The answer should come quickly and clearly: taking care of the house and our kids is extremely important, and he's the reason that I can be here.

Such a man is willing, if necessary, to put his own career on hold so that hers can flourish. That is a sacrifice he makes to support her and the family, just as she would support his decision if he chose to get a job. His job is likely to be part-time or have flexible hours to accommodate his family responsibilities, or perhaps he is able to work from home. Often, he will be thinking about the future and trying to keep his hand in a profession that he expects to further develop later in life. He will need a supportive partner who can fill in the gaps in child care and other household duties.

> **HOW CAN PARTNERS BEST SUPPORT EACH OTHER IN THEIR RESPECTIVE WORKPLACES AS THEY BUILD A THRIVING FAMILY LIFE TOGETHER?**

How can partners best support each other in their respective workplaces as they build a thriving family life together? Each needs the other's encouragement and understanding, day and night, both on-shift and off. Each requires workable solutions to the difficulties and frustrations that he or she faces daily.

THE PILLAR OF SOCIETY

For generations, society has expected that the woman will be the one who steps back from career ambitions. Increasingly, it is now the man. In his case, though, he is not so much stepping back as stepping up. He is standing up and coming forward to do what is right so that the woman he loves and supports can take her rightful place in the workplace and in society. He is learning that it is becoming socially acceptable to do what for so long has been considered by many to be women's duties.

The pillar of society needs constant maintenance to strengthen its support. Society can be very slow to recognize the groundswell that is taking place every day within families. That is because change, by its nature, starts in the small places. It is time we turned our attention to the big places to accomplish real change on a societal level. The millennial generation has become more willing to embrace differences, but outdated attitudes remain entrenched not only in individuals but also in our institutions.

> **IT IS TIME WE TURNED OUR ATTENTION TO THE BIG PLACES TO ACCOMPLISH REAL CHANGE ON A SOCIETAL LEVEL.**

How can we initiate a societal transformation to recognize the role of men supporting women? How can we provide boys with role models who show them that they are not less manly if they take the role of the homemaker? The answers to these questions will not be quick and easy. We have a long way to go. As responsible citizens who care about the society we leave for the next generation, we must step up, step forward, and step out—and, of course, lean on one another.

CHAPTER 1

SHRINKING
THE DISTANCES

FAMILY & SOCIETY PILLARS

In our global village, we seem closer together than ever, yet so far apart in our understanding of one another. Old attitudes linger in this age of diversity, which defines family in a variety of ways. To change society for the better, we must emphasize not what separates us but what we have in common.

*This chapter focuses primarily on the **pillars of family and society** as we take a long view of the state of today's relationships and the variety of family models in our modern culture. Society's slow evolution depends upon the strength of the other four pillars of support, and we will look at* *how they work together.*

Strolling with his grandmother in a village near Munich, my son, Dominik, who was three years old at the time, peered up at the gentleman who paused to greet them with a smile.

"A nice afternoon for a walk with your mom, isn't it?" the man said, winking.

"This is my grandma!" Dominik informed him, drawing closer to the woman holding his hand.

"Ah! I see. And where is your mom this fine day?"

"She's in Mumbai."

"And how about your dad? Is he in Mumbai, too?"

"No, no, he's in England."

"And where do you live?"

"Pittsburgh."

The gentleman tipped his hat and went on his way, still smiling, and more than a little confused. Dominik was telling the truth, though. That was his world, and it was both a big one and a small one. My wife, Mirka, and I had flown to Germany to leave him for a weekend visit with her parents. Then we each took separate flights— me to London, she to India—to attend to business responsibilities.

This is the life for so many families today. That scene was a decade ago, as I write this, and the world has continued to shrink in the years since. Neighborhoods extend across oceans and continents.

Mirka is a corporate executive who frequently is away from home. She devotes long hours to her career on behalf of our family. Meanwhile, I have attended to the needs of our children and to the complex duties of running our household. We followed her career from Germany to the United States and who knows where we will go next.

Her success gave the children and me the freedom and resources to explore. With our travel trailer, we twice toured America coast-to-coast. We wanted to learn as much as possible about a country that was new to us, a blend of cultures from around the world defining *family* in a variety of ways.

Many of those families are traditional: the husband is the primary breadwinner and the wife is the nurturer of the children and caretaker of the household. In other families, such as mine, those roles are reversed. In many families, both partners hold down jobs, either out of preference or necessity. In others, children grow up and learn about life with two dads, or two moms, some following the traditional roles and some redefining them. Every family finds its way.

To live in harmony and reach our potential, we must embrace changes and understand each other. Once we understand how much we have in common, we focus less on what separates us. That's true among nations, in the workplace, and in families. We can shrink the distances between us that at first can seem so hard to travel. We can reach out to one another in our global village.

That is why Mirka and I chose the name Globularity for the coaching business that we founded. Our experiences in life and in business have given us a perspective that we wish to share with others who are trying to navigate the complexities of their career and personal lives. We know how difficult it can be to juggle those responsibilities day by day, whether around the world or around the block.

We understand, because we have been there. We have identified the five pillars of support from the experiences of our own journey, and from listening closely to the experiences that hundreds of others have shared with us.

HEADS OF HOUSEHOLD

A common notion is that human beings are wired for the male to be the "head of household"—the provider and the decider—and for the female to be the nurturer who follows and supports. That is indeed many people's truth. But it's not true for all. The traditional roles and rules work well in some families, but others adopt different family models as new challenges and opportunities present themselves.

Women have long since established how well they can provide, as evidenced by the fact that, for years, they have outpaced men in receiving college degrees. In 1978, for the first time, more women than men earned associate degrees, according to data from the US Department of Education. Four years later, more women than men earned bachelor's degrees. In 1987, they took the lead in master's degrees, and starting in 2006, they began earning more doctorates.[2] As of 2018, women owned four of every ten businesses in the United States. The number of woman-owned businesses had increased 58 percent over a decade earlier, compared to only a 12 percent increase for businesses overall.[3]

MEN AREN'T LOSING THEIR PLACE. WOMEN ARE GAINING THEIRS.

Clearly, times are changing. The statistics aren't suggesting that men are getting lazy and letting the women take over the hard work. Men aren't losing their place. Women are gaining theirs. They are hitting their stride as equals alongside their male col-

---

2   Stanford University, *The College Puzzle*, blog, https://collegepuzzle.stanford.edu/tag/women-exceed-men-in-college-graduation/.

3   "Behind the Numbers: The State of Women-Owned Businesses in 2018," WBENC blog, https://www.wbenc.org/blog-posts/2018/10/10/behind-the-numbers-the-state-of-women-owned-businesses-in-2018.

leagues—and often ahead of them—as academics, entrepreneurs, and executives in the workplace. As women rise to ever greater stature in power and leadership, they are becoming role models for new generations.

Change brings more change in a ripple effect that is transforming society. This is not some competition that pits men against women. In truth, men have nothing to lose, but society has much to gain by tapping in to the full potential of women. When men and women collaborate, society reaps the benefits of their combined brain power. Together, as we build a strong structure with the five pillars of support, we accomplish more.

MEN HAVE NOTHING TO LOSE, BUT SOCIETY HAS MUCH TO GAIN BY TAPPING IN TO THE FULL POTENTIAL OF WOMEN.

Old attitudes linger, however. Many women feel guilty about their devotion to their career, as if that somehow means they are less devoted to family. They feel at times as if they are a bad mom, or a bad wife, and indeed, that is how some people, both men and other women, view them. Trying to live up to some idealized definition of womanhood, they endeavor to do it all. They try to be Superwoman but find that they cannot fly very well in a whirlwind.

Rarely has anyone of either sex achieved significant success in the business world while also single-handedly managing all the complex affairs of running a household: taking care of the kids, cleaning up, getting dinner on the table at six o'clock, paying the bills, managing the family social calendar. Breadwinners need support. If they pursue a demanding career, they might have to hire some of that support—by way of nannies and babysitters, housecleaners and cooks—but the presence of a loving parent cannot be replaced.

In many families today, the woman has been able to pursue career success because the man has stepped up to deal with the many challenges at home. He assumes the nurturing role that, historically, has been the female province. And if the woman's career aspirations call her to a different town or country, the man follows, even if he would prefer to stay. He does it lovingly for the sake of the family.

That is true leadership. It redefines *head of household* not as merely the moneymaker but as the homemaker as well. Still, a man who takes on those responsibilities might feel unmanly. He, too, can feel a sense of guilt: Why isn't he out making a living for the family? In truth, that is precisely what he is doing. He is supporting the woman to be all that she can be, to fully express her talents and reach her potential. He is providing the home that the family needs, and he's being a man about it.

LEANING IN, LEANING ON

In her 2013 bestseller *Lean In: Women, Work, and the Will to Lead,* Sheryl Sandberg, chief operating officer for Facebook, explores the challenges that women face as they try to forge ahead in their careers. "We stand on the shoulders of the women who came before us," she writes, "women who had to fight for the rights that we now take for granted." Despite women's advances, however, she points out that we have a long way to go: Men still run the world, she notes. Sexism, discrimination, and harassment still are rampant in the workplace.

The world appreciates successful men, Sandberg argues, but dislikes successful women. Though we all want to be liked, she says, women in leadership must understand that they can't please everyone if they want to change anything. Sandberg learned this lesson early and recommended that women take it to heart. They must turn a deaf ear to those who dismiss decisive and powerful women as "bossy."

Sandberg challenges women to rise up with the confidence and drive that men have long exhibited and to refuse to lower their expectations of success. We must encourage girls and young women to aspire to leadership, she writes, "to sit at the table, seek challenges, and lean in to their careers." Sandberg also founded LeanIn.Org, a foundation dedicated to supporting and inspiring women as they strive to achieve their goals. The book developed into a movement.

Sandberg describes her own struggles while balancing motherhood and career. She explains the importance of sharing with one's partner the responsibilities of parenting and managing the household. "A truly equal world," she writes, "would be one where women ran half our countries and companies and men ran half our homes."

No doubt about it: men certainly have the capacity to run households effectively and efficiently. I can say that with authority, as a man who has been running a household for years while his wife advances in her career. As women lean in to leadership, they need capable assistance. They need the kind of support at home that male leaders long have expected from their wives.

IT'S NOT IMPOSSIBLE TO HAVE IT ALL IF BOTH PARTNERS IN A RELATIONSHIP GIVE THEIR BEST.

Nothing is wrong with striving for both a successful career and a successful family life. They are not incompatible pursuits, and yet none of us is a superhero who can do it all. Still, it's not impossible to have it all if both partners in a relationship give their best.

Think of it this way: As a woman leans in to her career, who does she have to lean on? Does she have a partner who will be her pillar of support on their journey through life together as equals? For untold generations, men have leaned on the women in their lives to provide that loving partnership and support. Today, in our evolving society, women should be able to expect the same from men.

This does not put men in a position of subservience. A woman is not taking advantage of a man by leaning on him. Rather, she is elevating him. She is leveraging him for their collective success. When men fill the support role, they become servant leaders, rising to a new level of power and influence as they devote themselves to family, which, in the end, is what many people say matters most. Yes, men are natural providers. They simply have been discovering another way to show it.

IN PURSUIT OF HAPPINESS

I write this book to promote awareness of this evolving dynamic among couples trying to forge a life together. Although my focus will be on men and women, my words could just as well apply to partners of the same sex, because these are relational issues, not gender issues. Traditional families, too, will find much of value in these chapters because the fundamental theme here is universal and eternal: How can loved ones help each other to be their very best in the roles that they have taken on within their families?

It's time to both broaden and narrow the conversation. We must look not only at what women are facing as they strive to do well in the workplace but also at what men are facing as they strive to do well at managing the household. It comes down to the logistics, the practical steps that partners can take to help each other for the benefit of the family. How can men best support their women in the workplace? How can women best support the men at home? What steps should they take in the pursuit of happiness?

That is what we will explore in this book. The prevailing theme here is the need to understand and accept one another in our homes, in our workplaces, in our world. Each of us has strengths that we can bring to the fore so that we all benefit from living and loving and working in harmony. A deeper understanding can be the cure for so much of what ails our society, bringing us ever closer together. We each can do our part to shrink the distances. It's time to get started.

CHAPTER 2

THE PURPOSE
OF US

PARTNERSHIP, FAMILY
& SOCIETY PILLARS

This book's insights on supportive partnerships apply to a variety of family models and purposes, any of which can function well. To succeed, the partners must talk through their needs and dreams and discover what works best for them, while accepting what works for others.

*In this chapter, the predominant pillars that we examine are **partnership, family, and society.***

"Dad, do men need to work too?"

That was a quite simple yet revealing question from my three-year-old son as we waited in the car outside his mom's office building to pick her up after work. He was watching the afternoon stream of employees heading out to the parking lot, and he had noticed that many of them were men.

"Yes, Dominik, men go to work too," I explained to him. He seemed bewildered. "In many families," I continued, "it's the dad who goes off to work every day while the mom takes care of the kids."

His question surprised me. In our nontraditional family model, I had been prepared for a question such as, "Dad, why aren't you working too?" Dominik, though, was asking something else, something foundational. It wasn't about my role, specifically, but about the overall roles of men and women. His norm differed from the world of many other kids.

That was the moment when I realized that societal change was happening right in front of me. Our son, at such a tender age, had recognized that other families were built differently from his.

He would soon understand that our family model was one among a variety of possibilities, all of which can work well. Though the traditional family model may still be the norm, it does not define the norm. Our society includes a diversity of family purposes, each unique, including ours.

While I focus on supportive partnerships for women leaders in this book, many of these insights can be applied to all family models. I write this book for both the partner who gets a salary and for the partner who supports that wage earner and their children. It is for whoever is in those roles, whether male or female, married or unmarried, straight or gay. The pillars of healthy relationships apply to all.

I thought about trying to explain to Dominik that "making a living" involves both partners in a relationship, and that I, too, was making a living for our family by filling the role that traditionally has been the woman's. But he didn't need to hear all that. This was no time to deliver a discourse on the diversity of family models and purposes. My little boy just wanted to know that everything was okay.

I simply reassured him that it was just as normal for those men to go to work as it was for his mom to go to work. I turned to look at him in the back seat, where he had turned his attention back to his toys. *The day is coming so soon*, I thought, *when he will hear his playmates describing family scenarios unlike his own.* I wanted him to feel special but not different.

We could all use such reassurance. People tend to see life through the lens of their experiences, and we need to understand that other lifestyles are not the only possible option simply because we didn't grow up like that. Our options are not limited. In a way, we are all little children, watching people as they come and go and comparing ourselves to them. We learn, in time, that although many of them are very different from us, we have, nevertheless, much in common.

WE NEED TO UNDERSTAND THAT OTHER LIFESTYLES ARE NOT THE ONLY POSSIBLE OPTION SIMPLY BECAUSE WE DIDN'T GROW UP LIKE THAT.

As I write this, Dominik is twelve years old. His sister, Viktoria, is eight. Since the days when they were in diapers, their mom has kissed them goodbye and left for work each morning while their dad has stayed to tend to their daily needs.

Some would say that I am only a "stay-at-home" dad, although most days I am so busy running errands on behalf of our family that

I am not at home all that much. Women often wince when others describe them that way. The term feels dismissive and disrespectful. It seems to insinuate that those who devote themselves to caring for their homes and children should, instead, get up on their feet—as if they weren't on their feet all day long—and head out into the world to do something productive. This is why I prefer to be called Mr. Mom.

Good parenting is productive and very important because it prepares the next generation for success, but people define a good parent in different ways. Traditionally, the dad is a good parent if he earns a decent paycheck for his family, and the mom is a good parent when she focuses on the kids and the household. That model has functioned well for countless generations.

Other formulas, however, can be just as successful. Work is more than what you do to get a paycheck. Volunteers work, too, including those who volunteer to forgo a check to labor on behalf of their families. Working women—that is, women who earn a paycheck—are nothing new on the scene. For generations, women have been pursuing careers, and although they still face a host of challenges in a male-dominated workforce, many have attained positions of top leadership.

Not long ago, though, the career woman, as she was known, was an exception to the rule. She was seen to have stepped out of her normal place, which was presumed to be the home. Today, more men have been willing to step forward to support those women in the workforce in the way that those women have long supported them. Increasingly, as women rise to greater heights in their careers, it is the man who becomes caretaker of house and children.

It only makes sense. In many cases, women exceed men in their income potential, sometimes in multiples, and that is why they have assumed the role of breadwinner in so many families. As families work out their budgets, it seems unwise for the man to labor away at a job that yields little more than the cost of babysitters and day care. Why go to work for a meager salary and come home exhausted when, instead, you could be spending time with your kids? Why pay strangers to be surrogate parents?

This is not to presume that every family includes children, of course. Power couples, who both focus on their careers—one of Betsy Myers' three major family models—often have no children. The benefits of a cooperative arrangement extend to them as well, as they learn to be more supportive of each other and appreciative of the sacrifices that each makes for their mutual betterment. The principles are similar. Running a household involves a lot more than raising children, and power couples must learn to share those responsibilities so that each partner gets the support needed to focus on career.

MATTERS OF
THE HEART

An essential step for any couple, traditional or nontraditional, is for both partners to consider what they expect from the partnership. If they are considering an uncommon lifestyle that might be much different from what they observed growing up, how well will each adjust? We do not want to be captive to our childhood impressions, but we can't ignore them. If you grew up seeing your dad working hard at a job and your mom working hard around the house, would you be able to accept anything different from that?

The key here is open and frank communication from the onset. Successful couples say that essential to their thriving partnership are heartfelt talks about whether they can sustain an arrangement in which she builds a career and he takes care of the home and kids. Will he feel unmanly or emasculated? Will she feel unfeminine or somehow less of a lady? If he passes up a promotion, or steps aside from employment for a while, will he be happy with himself? If she can't spend as much time with her family, will she feel that she has failed in some way?

Those are matters of the heart, which can have everything to do with whether the partnership model will succeed. It's easy to say, "Just do what you have to do! Get over it!" True, many early concerns often prove to be unfounded. But what happens if one partner can't get over it, or won't? Then the whole endeavor, and possibly the relationship, is likely to fail. Too much is at stake. So talk about it.

Even after a couple decide to move forward in nontraditional roles, they will find it equally important to revisit the arrangement from time to time to make sure it still is working. By regularly taking their temperatures, both partners can prevent the sniffles from turning into the flu. Happiness is a reliable measure of success. If a partner feels out of sorts, the couple must never hesitate to ask why. Perhaps it's just a frustration of the moment, a reaction to the rigors of parenting or of a demanding job. Or perhaps it's something deeper in the heart that must be identified before it destroys.

BY REGULARLY TAKING THEIR TEMPERATURES, BOTH PARTNERS CAN PREVENT THE SNIFFLES FROM TURNING INTO THE FLU.

The cause of the friction can be internal or external. A couple might be in complete agreement on how to shape their partnership and family and yet encounter doubt, skepticism, and even outright opposition from others. It happened to Mirka and me. When we decided to switch the traditional roles, it was a defining time for us that challenged our relationships with close friends and family. After we married, for example, I decided to take her last name, rather than vice versa. My parents, family members, and many of our friends made it clear how they felt about that. My father, in fact, told me that he had expected to gain a daughter when I married, not lose a son. Naysayers are inevitable. A confident and supportive couple can resist them by finding strength in each other.

In our family, we regularly reevaluate our decisions to see whether we need to change course. We frequently move to new communities as Mirka advances in her career, and with each move we re-examine our lives and our state of happiness, and we talk openly with our children about it. They understand why moving is important. Still, it can be hard. When we relocated to Michigan, Dominik asked me, "Dad, will I be able to finish elementary school here?" I could only tell him, "I don't know." That has been a reality of our family life. Mirka and I have been honest with our kids about what to expect. We know that they will do best if they live under no illusions.

Our children also understand that their mom and dad have nontraditional roles, and they understand why. They understand that what works in their friends' families is not necessarily what will work in ours and that their friends are not somehow better than they are just because their mothers, not their fathers, see them off to school and make dinner for them every day.

Dominik and Viktoria find it perfectly normal that their mother is the one who earns the money to buy them the things that they need and want. They perceive their father as a natural nurturer, not as some awkward substitute. They know that we both love them and are acting in their best interest. They know their hearts are safe.

DEFINING
THE PURPOSE

In my coaching practice, I often ask clients a simple question to find out how much they have thought about their purpose and vision for life.

"Imagine yourself forty years from now," I say, "and you are sitting in a diner booth with a tall back separating you from the couple seated behind you. They are people you have known all your life. They don't know you're there, but you can hear their conversation—and they are talking about you.

"What will they be saying?" I ask my clients. "Is it what you would hope they will be saying about you?" As they consider that question, I ask them another one: "And what do you suppose they are saying about you right now?

In his book *Becoming Your Best: The 12 Principles of Highly Successful Leaders*, Steven R. Shallenberger shares simple but profound wisdom that includes developing a personal and family purpose. It is wisdom based on his decades of experience as an entrepreneur, CEO, corporate trainer, and community leader. He founded Synergy Companies, an industry leader in energy management and environmental solutions.

Shallenberger identifies and examines transformational principles shared by high achievers and organizations. Those who master those principles can enjoy sustainable health, happiness, and prosperity. They will develop trusting and enduring relationships. They will become the best they can be.

The principles for success are just as valid in the home as they are in the workplace. An essential step is to establish clear personal and family goals. What is your purpose as an individual and as a household leader? You can identify those objectives within several categories that are important to you—health, spirituality, family, career, community, and friends, for example.

How do you get started? Shallenberger suggests answering some fundamental questions aimed at developing your personal vision, such as: What drives you the most? What gets you excited? How would you describe your ideal lifestyle? Then identify the meaningful roles that you play in life, and describe how you perform at your best in each role—as the ideal parent, for example, or spouse, or business executive, or employee. Develop those goals clearly. Look for your full potential.

Each family member should define goals that are SMART—specific, measurable, achievable, realistic, and time specific. Your purpose and vision are longer-term goals for the next five to ten years. And each year you should have eight to twelve personal goals that will help you reach your long-term goals. Even kids as young as six years old should list lifetime goals. Although those no doubt will change, this is still a good exercise for children and helps them to feel they have a voice in the family. Our children have even made collages as a visual reminder of their goals. We hung them in the hallway as a daily reminder and encouragement. That way they won't resemble the New Year's resolutions that are forgotten within a month or two.

After establishing a personal purpose and goals, develop a family purpose and goals. How will you relate to your spouse and to your children? How do you envision your family life a decade from now, for example? Then break the family purpose and goals down into steps and, again, be time specific: Where will you be in five years? In a year? In a month? What can you do today to be closer to your goals tomorrow? Shallenberger suggests routinely reviewing progress on achieving those goals.

When defining your goals and purpose, imagine that you are plotting a road map on a journey. You are charting your destination, and although you know there will be detours and slowdowns along the way, you remain confident about where you are going. With your map close at hand, you can get back on course. Use your life and family purpose as the GPS to your happiness.

USE YOUR LIFE AND FAMILY PURPOSE AS THE GPS TO YOUR HAPPINESS.

As you develop your personal and family goals, write them down. Put your dreams on paper. That will make them seem more tangible and thus strengthen your intent to pursue them. Life gets busy. Dreams can fade amid the daily parade of responsibilities. The key is to give priority to your vision so that everything falls into place in fulfilling it.

Perhaps you have always wanted to start your own company by the time you are forty years old. Write down that objective and put it where you will often see it, as a reminder. When you do, ask yourself what steps you have taken toward that end. If you keep it top of mind, it will be far more likely to come true.

When you have a master plan for yourself and for your family, you and your loved ones can revisit it regularly. At least once a year, take stock. Dreams and objectives can change, particularly after major life events such as the birth of a child, a major promotion, or a move to a new community. Don't let it all just happen. Make sure that it happens intentionally. You can always decide to set your sights on a new destination, but don't get lost on a detour.

Each year between Christmas and New Year's, Mirka, the kids, and I sit down and take a look at the goals and purposes for each individual as well as the family. Each of us takes another look at what is important to us individually and collectively. We each make our own list, and then we compare them. Based on what we discover, we reconsider our destination and the next steps on our journey. We look for areas of agreement and disagreement and whether we need to find a compromise for the sake of a unified family purpose.

For example, I might contribute this: Next year, I see myself continuing as the supporting spouse, with primary responsibility for taking care of our home and our children. However, I would like to postpone moving again at least until our children have finished middle school. I recently stated that I would like to write a book about us—both a personal and a family goal—and that objective, as readers can see, made it into our plan as well.

PLANNING TOOLS

As you consider where you want to go in life and how to track your goals, there are a variety of resources and tools available.

For our annual goals, Mirka and I use the Full Focus Planner developed by Michael Hyatt. It keeps us on track toward those goals on a daily, weekly, and monthly basis: https://fullfocusplanner.com/

For our children, we use the Big Life Journal planner: https://biglifejournal.com/

While each of us pursues our personal goals, we must also consider the needs of the other and the family so that our pursuits advance all of us rather than set us back. We are stronger when we tackle life together. We are greater than the sum of our parts.

I have learned that couples who are considering a nontraditional arrangement, or who are already engaged in one, should not make assumptions about each other's goals and ambitions. They need to be aware of visions that are not in alignment as soon as possible and make any necessary course corrections. At every step, couples should examine the logistics and continue talking through the details.

Failure to do so can have severe consequences. Marriages fall apart. Families unravel. Dreams recede and vanish. What sometimes happens is that one partner or the other, or both, will sink into silence to keep the peace. Perhaps these partners feel they are being selfish by sharing personal ambitions when the family has so many pressing needs and concerns. They tell themselves that their day will come, but without a vision of that day, and some idea of when it will be, resentments take root. Couples begin to argue over seemingly trivial matters. A dirty dish left in the sink elicits not a shrug but a screech.

THE TEAM CANNOT WIN UNLESS ALL THE PLAYERS ARE AT THEIR BEST, WORKING TOGETHER ON THE SAME OBJECTIVE.

The real problem is a dream deferred. A lack of communication is the illness, and the cure can come with a sharing of hearts, some words of reassurance, and a clearly defined, written purpose for the family and everyone in it. The team cannot win unless all the players are at their best, working together on the same objective.

The children, of course, are part of that team. In many families, the planning centers on them, with the prime consideration being their welfare and growth into productive, happy citizens. Although Dominik and Viktoria are still too young to understand a lot of life's complexities, Mirka and I are very open with them and try to integrate them in family matters. They don't call the shots, of course, but we let them know what's going on, even before we have reached a final decision. We let them know when we are considering moving, and we talk to them about vacation plans and what they would like to do. We don't spring surprises on them. We make no assumptions about how they feel. We encourage them to tell us.

SACRIFICE AND REWARDS

At the moment, one focus of our family principles is to do whatever is required for Mirka to move forward in her career while raising our two children to reach their full potential and prepare them for a changing world. If her job requires us to move again, we will do so. Ultimately, we are seeking to use each of our talents to provide the best support possible for our children. As we weigh our daily decisions, we must be willing to sacrifice, as necessary, for the greater cause. We do what we must do to fulfill our goals.

Mirka, without a doubt, would like to spend more time with our children, enjoying more of the traditional mom time with them. She misses out on many of those family hours so that she can provide for us abundantly with the resources that support our lifestyle. Meanwhile, part of me would like more time to myself and to develop my own pursuits, but my wife and children need me where I am. I enjoy serving in this way and am grateful for the opportunity to contribute meaningfully to a thriving family, but I, like Mirka, am weighing advantages and disadvantages and abiding by our purpose.

Mirka understands that she can't have it all. I understand that I can't, either. Together, though, we can come a whole lot closer to that ideal than either of us could hope to achieve alone. In our marriage, the two are one. We put our hearts and minds together. Her strengths complement my strengths as we strive to become our best. We gain far more than we lose. As each of us sacrifices, the family grows.

In fact, the rewards have been so plentiful along the way that we scarcely think of what we are doing as sacrificing. It's true that our children certainly haven't been delighted at the prospect of moving every few years, but it's also true that they will not have to worry about how to finance their college education. They travel to places that other kids have not even heard about. Our family lifestyle teaches them to be adaptable, to accept other cultures, and cultivate a mindset of growth. (For more information about the concept of a growth mindset, see chapter 6.) We can give them experiences and advantages that many children lack, and that is their reward for not always having Mom around and having to put up with Dad.

Personally, I reap rewards in the form of freedom and choices. Though my household duties keep me hopping, I do not need to report to a daily job, thanks to Mirka's career success. I have been gifted with the precious commodity of time. It is my responsibility to use it well. Some people in my position choose to homeschool their children. Others launch businesses or become active volunteers in their communities. Some develop fascinating and perhaps lucrative hobbies. This book is one such manifestation of the rewards of our lifestyle. No way would I have had the time to author it if I had been locked into a work day consuming much of my waking hours.

STEPPING BACK, STEPPING UP

In a sense, the sacrifices involved in running a family will require both partners to step back, at least for a time, from what they might otherwise wish to pursue. They should both have some idea about how long they will continue in that role and should speak up if the arrangement at any point seems unfair or unworkable. Neither partner should feel as if he or she is doing all the sacrificing. Establishing a time frame helps to clarify matters. If the arrangement is indefinite by agreement, that understanding should be specified in the family plan. It should not go unspoken.

In our case, I have stepped back from employment to devote myself as the primary family caretaker. At first, when we were still in Germany and learned that Mirka was pregnant, we figured that I would take care of our baby full-time until we could put day care arrangements in place or, perhaps, until he was no longer in diapers. Then, when her career brought us to the United States, we anticipated that I would need to manage our household for three to five more years as her work shifted us to various locations. I have continued in that role considerably longer than we had anticipated.

We are not just letting this happen, however. We talk about it. Whenever we have decided to extend my responsibilities as chief caretaker, we have done so for clear reasons. I have not simply acquiesced to this role. I have chosen it. We started with a plan, and we have continued with one even as life's uncertainties and opportunities have pointed us in new directions. It's all part of the journey.

Mirka, meanwhile, has been stepping back, too, even as her career has been full speed ahead. She cannot be present with our family as often as she would like to be. She primarily exhibits her deep devotion to us in a different way, as the family breadwinner, and yet it is human nature to desire more time with the people you love. We do our best to ensure that every hour she has with us is meaningful, but she feels torn nonetheless. The mind says one thing, the heart another.

Although stepping back is what each of us is doing in a literal sense, I prefer to think of our arrangement as stepping up. We are rising to the challenge in a true partnership. Together we have defined a family model for ourselves and for our children that will allow us to build toward an ever more prosperous, happy, and fulfilled future. It's not the model that works for everyone. It's the one that works best for us.

CHAPTER 3

RUNNING A FAMILY IS LIKE RUNNING A BUSINESS

PARTNERSHIP, FAMILY & SELF PILLARS

To run smoothly, a family needs systems in place, a clear delegation of responsibilities, and methods for measuring performance. In other words, it should be set up much like a successful business.

*The primary pillars in this chapter are **partnership, family, and self**.*

"Thank you very much, sir," the waiter said as he set the check on the table in front of me. Then he turned to Mirka and presented her with a small cardboard box. "And this is for the leftovers if you would like to take them home."

This is a typical scene when my wife and I dine out, and it happened again as I was writing this chapter. As the restaurant staff sees it, this is the norm: The man's role is to be the breadwinner and provider, while the woman's domain is all things domestic. Most couples expect the man to get the check and might even be annoyed if the waiter were to give it to the woman.

Mirka winked at me and slid the box to my side of the table as I slipped a credit card into the folder with the check. Neither of us takes offense at such sex-role assumptions. That's just the way of the world, and nothing is wrong with social gestures such as that. Those assumptions, however, are based on traditional gender roles that often do not apply to families today. They also are rooted in personal convictions about who should do which job—that is, men's work versus women's work. Some couples even feel that anything other than those standards is somehow unromantic, as if they compromise the meaning of masculinity and femininity.

Such expectations work for some, but for many, they are outdated and simply don't align with an emancipating society and workforce. It is sweet that a man opens a door for a woman if she finds that to be romantic, but should that gesture extend to informing her that she should stay home while he is out earning a living? Should he not also open the door for her to find career satisfaction? And if she does choose the family caregiver role, should her husband not acknowledge that she is earning their living that way too?

I do not feel unmanly in my role as our family's chief financial officer and domestic affairs supervisor, and nor does Mirka feel unfeminine in her role as chief career developer and fund-raiser. To the contrary, we feel that we are fulfilling purposes to which we are well suited, and we know that our roles, though essential, do not define us. Mirka cares about our children and home life every bit as much as I do, even though I am primarily responsible for the planning. And I care about Mirka's career as much as she does, because I want her to fulfill her potential and because her income opens so many possibilities for all of us. Each of us is contributing selflessly toward our mutual betterment and our children's future.

In many ways, running a family is like running a business. Each is an organization in which the right people need to be in the right jobs. As must a well-run business, a well-run family must operate efficiently, with decisions made rationally rather than emotionally. Families and businesses thrive when they are pursuing a distinct purpose, not just drifting along aimlessly, or only focused on paying the bills.

A WELL-RUN FAMILY MUST OPERATE EFFICIENTLY, WITH DECISIONS MADE RATIONALLY RATHER THAN EMOTIONALLY.

To excel, organizations need effective leadership and clear delegation of duties and responsibilities. Most people these days would agree that businesses should base their hiring decisions on the best person for the job, not on whether it is a man's job or a woman's job. Quite simply, there is work to be done by whoever is in a position to do it.

I am not saying that emotions don't matter. I certainly am not suggesting that a family should be run with a cold precision that treats people as if they were interchangeable parts of a machine. That would destroy a family culture, just as it would destroy a business culture. Efficiency must come with compassion. Love and caring hold families together. They are essential elements in the pillars of support.

Still, family decision making needs to reflect the sort of business savvy that does not shy away from tough decisions for the long-term health of the organization. If the woman has the bigger paycheck and the more promising career, her husband should encourage her and assume a fair share of household responsibilities. He may choose to work only part-time or perhaps postpone his own career ambitions to focus on running the household. He may not prefer it that way, but in a well-functioning family he will do so anyway, for a time at least, for the greater good. Countless women have made that sacrifice, and men must be willing to do so, too, when circumstances call for it. The heart might say one thing, but the facts of the situation call for a different approach.

When the purpose and the goals are clear, as we discussed in chapter 2, a family can move forward without becoming mired in indecision and emotion. When they see they're progressing toward their destination, family members can enjoy the trip, despite the bumps along the road. That's why it is so essential for couples to know where they are going and why. Once they have that out in the open, they can more readily take on nontraditional responsibilities, having agreed upon what they mutually wish to accomplish. Husband and wife together become servant leaders, dedicated to each other's happiness and the ultimate success of their family. That is the sort of leadership, in fact, that characterizes many successful businesses.

The business of running a family isn't easy. To do it right, you need to plan meticulously, setting budgets and schedules and meeting deadlines and quotas. There are tasks and projects to organize and complete and resources to manage and allocate. It takes dedication and persistence in the tough as well as in the good times, to build for future prosperity. Nobody would doubt that's true for running a business; it is equally true for running a family.

GETTING DOWN
TO BUSINESS

First, let's look at a couple of tools that can help a family operate more efficiently, more as a business would operate. Efficiency is not a bad word. It does not imply a sterile lifestyle where everything must be done by the book. Instead, efficiency avoids the waste that can suck away family resources. One of those resources is money, which, when used wisely, buys freedom and opens up opportunities. Another is time, the most precious of all riches, which, when squandered, is gone forever.

SYNC THE CALENDARS

In managing our household, I operate several separate online calendars: one for me, one for each of our two children, one for the dogs, one for household chores and responsibilities, and one for our travels. I use the Google calendar service. I can overlay and sync those schedules as needed to see our overall schedule and ensure that we can work out any conflicts.

Mirka has a calendar, as well, which includes her business scheduling and trips, but I don't sync hers with the others. It is filled with highly detailed information that is much more involved than what I need for managing the household. She needs it, clearly, but all I need are the times when she will be away, where she will be, and any flight numbers and hotel rooms that she has booked. I include this information in my calendar for planning purposes.

Meanwhile, Mirka can open the master calendar to see what the family plans are for today, for next week, for next month, and beyond. She can find out at a glance where our children will be in their activities. She can quickly see when would be a good time to call me or the children. We might agree in advance that the hour before dinner, for example, would be convenient.

Some people rebel at elaborate scheduling, preferring to do things spontaneously. That's nice, unless that spontaneity conflicts with somebody else's schedule. Nobody in the business world would get along with colleagues by discounting the value of their time. It doesn't work in a family setting, either. It's not as if you cannot schedule plenty of free time as well. Everyone needs time to relax, time to just go with the flow. To be free spirited is wonderful, so long as you are not aimless and oblivious to commitments. By blocking off personal time on your calendar, you still can be sensitive to the needs of others.

> **TO BE FREE SPIRITED IS WONDERFUL, SO LONG AS YOU ARE NOT AIMLESS AND OBLIVIOUS TO COMMITMENTS.**

PROJECT MANAGEMENT

Anyone who has been involved in project management and also tried to run a household effectively understands the similarity between the two. Fortune 500 companies and start-ups alike have found that an app called Trello can be quite helpful for organizing and prioritizing information and tasks. This project management tool also works well for managing family activities.

For on-the-job project management, the app lets you set up various checklists, boards, and cards that you can share with your team. It is quite helpful for keeping track of the many aspects of a complicated project. Household planning is not necessarily any less multifaceted.

In my family, for example, we set up our Christmas celebration as a project on the app, including categories for decorations, Christmas cards, and presents. It keeps both Mirka and me informed about what the other is taking on so that we can make the most of our time and not duplicate efforts. On Trello, we list the presents that we anticipate purchasing for the children, and whoever buys an item, either online or in a store, can checkmark it and automatically send a notification so that we can easily keep track of who has done what. The holidays can get manic, as many families know only too well. Planning can bring tranquility back to the season, and technology can make preparations and communication efficient and therefore all the easier.

We use the Trello tool for a variety of functions, whether they are elaborate family projects or simply booking a hotel room for vacation. In fact, we can pull up a list of things to pack by simply calling up a list that we prepared for a similar vacation in a previous year. Most families, I'm sure, would confess to starting from scratch each year, jotting down items on a scrap of paper and then losing that scrap of paper. The Trello app keeps it all organized and just a click or two away from future reference.

DEALING WITH MONEY

As any business must, a family must figure out how to manage money and cash flow. There are many views on how to manage family financials—combined accounts, separate accounts, or a mix, for example—and when I talk to couples about such matters, I make it clear that those decisions are up to them. I am not a professional financial planner.

In our family, we have a combined financial model. All our accounts are joint, and we both have full access to them. As a strategic decision, we made me the CFO, but I keep Mirka apprised of where we stand and where the money is going. I don't bother her with all the details. She doesn't have time for that. Still, she certainly cares about our family's financial health, so I provide her with an overview every two weeks and with a cash-flow model every quarter. I handle all the details, and I keep her in the loop with those regular briefings. That way she can fully participate in the major decisions influencing our financial direction. She receives all the information and background she needs to discern whether all is well or whether it is time to change course. We have found that approach works well in our family.

JUST THE FACTS, PLEASE

C-suite executives do not inform their colleagues of every detail of their interactions. In a complex organization, that would lead to a maddening information overload. Staff members limit themselves to reporting the results of their delegated tasks. Each of them shares with the others what they need to know to operate effectively and to address their mutual concerns. The CEOs look primarily at big picture issues. Ideally, they trust their managers to do their jobs, without excessive supervision or need for micromanagement.

Too much information can clutter the vision and get in the way of seeing the big picture. If my wife and I were to compare notes on everything we do, we likely would forget the most important things.

I make the decisions involved in running the household, but in certain cases, consulting as a couple is appropriate. I will not make major decisions unilaterally. Mirka deserves and appreciates the opportunity to participate. On some matters that I understand to be especially meaningful to her, I will defer to her to make the decision, though I still offer my viewpoint.

I present what she needs to know clearly and concisely, in consideration of her time constraints. As a busy executive, her calendar is full and her mental bandwidth is crowded. I give her the most important facts, just as she would expect her colleagues to do when making a business decision. I lay out the particulars of the situation, whether it's a major purchase that we are considering or a problem that we must solve. I present some options or solutions along with the pros and cons of various choices. I give her an overview to help her make an informed decision. Addressing such matters efficiently saves us valuable family time.

Clear communication is essential, but like virtually anything, it has its limits. If we determine the need to thoroughly talk about something, such as a situation with the kids, a family project, or an investment, we often set a time limit on our discussion and stick to it, as if we were running a business meeting and needed to respect everyone's time. We are looking for balance. Neither of us wishes to cut short meaningful conversation, and we certainly will devote the necessary time to whatever is on our agenda. As with any agenda, however, we must set a pace and work through the items methodically. Otherwise we might never get to other important matters that also merit attention.

KEY PERFORMANCE INDICATORS

In the corporate world, key performance indicators (KPIs) help executives evaluate their progress on achieving important objectives. The indicators are measurable data that may focus on overall performance, or on specific business processes and goals within departments. For example, how many sales contracts were signed in the last quarter? What was the growth in revenue? Did the total of accounts receivable change significantly? When you go by the numbers, it's easier to assess progress or see early signs of trouble. KPIs allow everyone to be aligned around the goals of the business and to know whether we are winning or losing.

Families can have their own KPIs to determine whether they are on track with their family purpose or of there is a need to make changes. For example, from year to year we monitor our children's grades in school. We are not looking so much at whether the grades are As or Cs—though, obviously, we encourage excellence—but rather, at whether the As turned to Cs over the course of the year. Grades can be an indicator of something going on in a child's life. A significant dip in grades can cue parents to look for a possible cause. It might be a serious issue, such as depression or bullying. It could be something easily resolved such as spending less time with a new boyfriend or girlfriend, for example, or with video games, or even with sports.

Children's performance in sports also can serve as a valuable KPI. Is the child improving, going sideways, or slipping? Because of Mirka's career requirements, our family has frequently moved. After every move, our children began performing less well at sports. We determined that it was a normal reaction as they adjusted to the new environment, and they soon regained their balance. Nonetheless, we needed to be watchful. It's when you're not looking that so much can go wrong.

The family calendar itself can serve as a KPI. Is everyone able to abide by the schedule, or is it often ignored or superseded? Does the pace of life seem frantic or reasonably relaxed? If your calendar keeps track of individual and family goals, are you making progress on achieving them, or do they seem further away than when you wrote them down?

Is the family budget where you want it to be? Are you reaching your goals? Your financial performance is another KPI to watch closely. You do not need to count every receipt, but you should watch for patterns. By setting specific objectives for your savings and investments, you can easily compare the numbers currently in your accounts to the numbers that you projected. If they don't come close, then you do have a lot to talk about, such as saving more, spending less, and setting priorities. If you expect a prosperous future, you must begin planning for it long in advance. By keeping a budget that tallies income and expenses, you will be able to track the family cash flow and look for areas to improve.

Couples may want to consider KPIs that can reveal much about the health of their relationship. Emotions aside, what do the numbers say about the state of the marriage—for example, how often you go out on a date or how often you fight? You might not feel inclined to mark fights on your calendar, but at least consider the frequency of positive and negative interactions. You may have to free yourself of stress and tension that is harming your relationship. You may need to learn new ways to handle conflict. Sometimes the biggest step is acknowledging that your relationship is suffering. If you are in denial, you are unlikely to seek the help that can put you back on track to romance.

As you track your KPIs, keep in mind the Shallenberger principles that we discussed in chapter 2. His book, and website (www. becomingyourbest.com) are valuable resources for developing life goals and leadership skills, and for staying on track with what you and your family have resolved to accomplish. In addition, the Full Focus Planner calls for a weekly review of those accomplishments, and the Big Life Journal includes ways to track stress and random acts of kindness. All can be useful as KPIs.

Things that you can measure are easier to grasp and understand. KPIs can transform complex issues into concrete data that you can control. They communicate the underlying health of the organization, whether that's a business or a family. You might not like what you learn, but at least you will know what is happening so you can take action. Those who know are more likely to do.

A SAMPLING OF KPIS

CHILDREN'S GRADES IN SCHOOL

CHILDREN'S SPORTS PERFORMANCE

PROGRESS ON ESTABLISHED GOALS

FAMILY FINANCIAL PERFORMANCE

FAMILY BUDGET ADHERENCE

FREQUENCY OF ARGUMENTS

FREQUENCY OF DATE NIGHTS

ACTS OF KINDNESS

STRESSFUL SITUATIONS

EFFECTIVE FEEDBACK

Business professionals agree that feedback from customers, partners, and employees is critical to drive continuous improvement and a valuable resource to optimize operations. Through surveys, social media, and other methods, companies try to take the pulse of the people whom they serve and who serve them. Their goal is to improve both the customer experience and the company culture. Ideally, they are doing much more than setting up forums for airing grievances. They are soliciting solutions and identifying trends. A company that proves to be the best at serving customers will topple the competition.

That's how it should be in the family setting too. Feedback is an opportunity to learn and promote a mindset of growth. All family members need to be heard. One way to ensure they get that opportunity is to establish a weekly or daily get-together—sometimes called the Monday huddle—at which family members briefly update one another, talk about plans for the upcoming days or weeks, and share any concerns.

These conversations, which we schedule a few times a week, often include plenty of feedback. We talk about the past few days and how our plans have progressed. We refer to our calendars to see where we have been and where we are going.

When you have these discussions, avoid straying into emotional asides. That can be hard to do when comparing what was planned with what was accomplished. This isn't the time to air grievances. It doesn't help to scowl and make comments such as "Why can't you keep your promise to get home on time for dinner?" or "I see you didn't bother to clean up the garage!" Getting angry accomplishes nothing.

This is an update, not an inquest. Reminders are good. Nagging is bad. If anyone needs to do better, the facts alone will make that clear as you review them during the family huddle. Conversation collapses when you put others on the defensive or attack their character. The result can be a quarrel between two people, or squabbling among the entire family. Conflict of that sort hardly qualifies as feedback, and it does not encourage productivity. Instead, let the facts speak for themselves, and understand what can get in the way of good intentions. Revise the family schedule if necessary, with reasonable expectations that will work for everyone.

HIRING, FIRING, OUTSOURCING

When people aren't working out well on the job, they may need further training or the right tools. If those resources don't work, transference to a different position may better suit their abilities and inclinations. To let ineffective people keep plugging away ineffectively is unfair to everyone. When all else fails, it's time to say, "You're fired!"

FAMILY MATTERS WILL NOT ALWAYS PROCEED LIKE CLOCKWORK. THE STANDARD SHOULD BE EXCELLENCE, NOT PERFECTION.

I'm not saying you should kick anyone in your family to the curb, but it is hard to tolerate consistent failure to perform a crucial job. The family's well-being depends on getting it done, so it is time for a firing and a hiring. To put it more gently, think of it as a job transfer.

Family matters will not always proceed like clockwork. The standard should be excellence, not perfection. The family culture should be encouraging and understanding. Let's say that a family's circumstances change and the wife gets a new job with long hours. She no longer has time to do all the grocery shopping. Meanwhile, the husband, though just as busy, has a flexible work schedule. It's time for that job transfer. He's hired! Or perhaps he breaks a leg and can't mow the lawn. Who mows it now? It will either be her or someone else.

Smart businesses outsource. They do not presume that they can fulfill every function effectively. Others can do certain jobs faster, cheaper, and better. If the task is not core to the company's purpose, management can bring in hired help. Some companies outsource their human resources function, for example. They may rely on an accounting firm rather than an in-house bookkeeper. The boss probably isn't interviewing candidates for staff janitor. Rather, the company hires a cleaning firm.

Smart families outsource too. What is the value of your time? Unless you love shoveling the snow from the driveway, why would you do it when you can hire a neighborhood kid for $10? You save an hour of backbreaking work, and it's likely that the value of your labor is worth more than $10 an hour.

A well-functioning family will take stock of who is better at which tasks. If any task is not core to the family's purpose, then bring in hired help. Some couples make the same mistake that some businesses make: They try to do it all, and they can't. They think that they are striving to be productive and efficient, but they end up feeling frustrated and exhausted, wondering why they never seem to have time for what matters most. Overworked entrepreneurs can get to the point where they forget why they got into their business in the first place. They lose sight of their passions. It happens in families too. No need for that when plenty of folks will eagerly do those odd jobs.

Husbands and wives often will disagree on the relative importance of a certain task or the standards that should be maintained when performing that task. That is not surprising, considering they are different people with different perspectives. Neither is necessarily right or wrong. I consider myself to be reasonably tidy, but I am not particularly bothered by toothpaste spots on the bathroom mirror. Mirka hates them, so for her sake I tried to keep the mirror spotless, but we found the best solution was hiring a cleaner. We outsourced.

Sometimes, a couple may decide to keep doing a job that easily could be outsourced. I have never minded mowing the lawn, but with everything else I am juggling, the grass often gets shaggy. I suggested to Mirka that it was time to hire a lawn service. "Well," she said, "I've been thinking about that. I've been wanting to exercise more, and that would be a good way for me to do it." So, she found that mowing the grass was a way to fulfill one of her personal goals. Again, it's a matter of perspective. We decided to fire me and hire her for the job.

However, after several weeks, she too found that she couldn't keep up with the mowing, because of her busy schedule. So, we recruited a boy from the neighborhood. Our plans hadn't worked, but the outsourcing option was always there. This had nothing to do with gender role. We don't define responsibilities as a man's work or a woman's work. First, I pushed the lawnmower; then she did. Then neither of us did. The one who does a job should be determined by the one who is best suited for it, who has more time for it, who gives it a higher priority, and who wants to do it. When none of that works out, outsourcing is the answer.

It often has been said that time is money, but it is more than that. Yes, we should do things as efficiently as possible not only to save money but also to have more quality time to spend with loved ones. Financial resources are critical to manage properly, but togetherness is also an important resource to foster.

Mirka suggested once that she would like to spend time with our daughter, Viktoria, by taking her to her tennis lessons. A wonderful thought, but I offered another perspective. "Honey, I'm concerned that you'll be stuck in traffic on the way there," I said, "and then the whole time she's practicing, you won't be able to talk to her much. Maybe, instead, you could take that time to get some of your work done, and then, this weekend, do something special with her where you can really get a chance to talk." In essence, I was recommending that she outsource herself. By shifting some priorities, she was able to open precious time for their togetherness.

THE RIGHT PEOPLE IN THE RIGHT JOBS

In their hiring practices, businesses strive to get the right people in the right jobs. It's only common sense. The most-qualified people should be hired for jobs to which they are well suited. Often, problems arise when it's time for those folks to get promotions. They find themselves in a new position with responsibilities unlike anything they have previously experienced.

Let's say that Mary, a young computer programmer, shows such promise that her company decides to reward her by putting her in charge of an IT team. Suddenly, the rising star is fading. Mary has no experience in managing others, nor is she a born leader. The way she sees it, she was doing what she loved to do until she did it so well that she wasn't allowed to do it anymore. Mary figured it would be career suicide to turn down a promotion, and so she was set up for failure.

What happens in a company can happen in a family. Couples need to make sure that they each are handling the responsibilities appropriate for them. In many families, they just fall into certain roles with which they are not a good fit. Those roles might seem to make sense at the time, but at some point, the couple should evaluate them. Otherwise, frustrations will set in and the couple may find themselves bickering. If he is meticulous about how the dishes should be stacked in the cabinet, and she has a more freestyle approach, why would it make sense for that job to fall to her? Because she's the woman? If he hates to get his hands dirty and she loves to garden, why should it be his job to spread the fertilizer? Because he's the man?

Such frustrations are unnecessary. With a little planning, couples can divvy up the duties in a way that works for both of them. There is always room for improvement. Try this every day for a week: Keep a notebook in your pocket and write down your household chores and the areas of responsibility that fall to you. Ask your spouse to do the same. Then compare notes on the weekend, and talk about whether the way you have split the roles makes sense. You may not see a need for a wholesale change in those roles, but you likely will see opportunities to tweak them to better suit your personalities and circumstances.

KEEP IN MIND THE FULL BREADTH OF YOUR SPOUSE'S CONTRIBUTIONS TO THE FAMILY, AND BE SURE TO OFFER ENCOURAGEMENT AND THANKS.

Through it all, be appreciative of each other's efforts. Even as you work to streamline the division of duties, beware of any feelings of resentment that you are doing most of the work. You aren't. Keep in mind the full breadth of your spouse's contributions to the family, and be sure to offer encouragement and thanks. And then get down to the business of fine-tuning. The right people in the right jobs will get things done more efficiently, and efficiency buys that precious time for you and your loved ones to share.

WHO CALLS THE SHOTS?

In any organization, a time will come when the leadership disagrees on how to proceed. Generally, a team of business executives with solid credentials and plenty of experience might get along well, but they are individuals with different outlooks. Opinions will differ, as they should. The leaders should feel free to speak their mind, holding one another accountable, and not simply nod in agreement. Healthy debate often produces better options. Nonetheless, somebody still has to be the ultimate arbiter.

The CEO generally makes the call at such times. Though the CEO delegates a lot of the decision making to others on the team—the COO, CFO, and such—the corporate structure determines who outranks whom, and the CEO sits at the top. As the caretaker of the company's purpose and vision, the top executive is expected to decide the course of action that will best advance that vision.

In a family organization, decision making is a similar process, though generally less authoritarian. When the leadership—that is, husband and wife—disagrees on how to proceed, they need to review the family purpose and vision and how they have agreed to delegate responsibilities. If they disagree on a matter, they should determine which of them is offering a solution that is more in keeping with their overall objectives. If they each seem to have a reasonable solution, then the decision of the spouse who bears the primary responsibility for the matter in question should prevail.

In other words, the line of command will depend upon the family model that the couple has adopted and their agreement on who handles which responsibilities. Each spouse must respect the other's realm of authority. They shouldn't get in each other's way.

In my family, if Mirka and I are not in sync on an issue involving the children or the running of the household, then I will make the final call. She understands that I am more in tune with our domestic needs. However, she will make the final call on issues involving her travel and career needs. If she were to say, "I have been transferred and we must move next month," I would not insist that we stay. She knows what is best for her career, and I understand that the income from her career in large part defines our lifestyle.

Still, the nature of a loving relationship calls for more delicate discussions than are usually necessary in a corporate setting. A couple's decision-making style is likely to be collaborative and consultative. In a healthy relationship, each partner is a servant leader. Together they take decisive actions, each keeping the other's interests top of mind as well as what is best for their children.

Deference is not weakness. It demonstrates the strength of commitment. True leadership is not a matter of who gets to call the shots. Wise CEOs will not act on a whim but, instead, will defer to the company purpose, the founding principles, the company's vision. A wise couple does not engage in a power struggle. They agree on how to disagree. In our family, some decisions will be mine, and some will be Mirka's, but really, neither of us calls the shots. Together, we defer to our family purpose as the guiding authority, and then everything falls into place.

GETTING GOOD ADVICE

Strong people solicit the advice of trusted mentors. They do not presume to know it all, and that humble awareness often leads them to learn more. An executive hoping to get to the next career level can seek assistance in a variety of ways, such as from a consultant, trainer, or coach. Consultants offer instruction on what to do, based on their expertise in a specific field. Trainers can help executives, or the staff in general, do better with certain skills, such as improving sales through proven techniques and systems. Coaches help people understand themselves so that they can mature in their leadership skills and accelerate their pursuit of excellence.

Personality tests can be quite revealing. In my coaching, for example, I use the StrengthsFinder assessment developed by the Gallup analytics and advice firm. By asking dozens of questions about preferences and attitudes, the assessment helps individuals to identify areas of strength and weakness that can have an impact on their career choices. Once again, awareness is the first step to improvement. You can't get started until you know what you don't know.

Many excellent books offer valuable advice on improving business skills, performance, and leadership, or on running a family more efficiently or kick-starting a faltering marriage. They cannot help you, though, unless you read them and put their wisdom into practice. Only those who are determined to pursue excellence are likely to find it. Advisors can give you the tools for success and help you to see your potential, but it's up to you to take it from there.

CHAPTER 4

EMPOWERING
YOUR PARTNER

PARTNERSHIP PILLAR

As the partners work out their roles in a relationship, each must take care to empower the other. Once they decide who will handle which responsibility, each partner must be allowed to undertake that responsibility as he or she sees fit, without interference from the other. Yet, the lines of communication must stay wide open for discussions about mutual dreams and, if necessary, a reassessment of the family model.

The pillar of partnership is the focus of this chapter. This is primarily about how the partners develop and maintain a supportive relationship.

"My husband is doing everything wrong!" our friend exclaimed, throwing up her arms in dismay. Mirka and I had met her for lunch, and it was clear that she needed to talk. She and her husband (we'll call them Donna and Bill) recently had begun a way of life that was new to them but familiar territory for us.

After sixteen years of running the household and homeschooling their five children, Donna had wanted to refocus on her career, and she and Bill decided together that now was the time. During those years, Bill had built a successful business. He had recently sold it, and now he was supporting his family in a different way: he was turning his attention to the house and kids while Donna took her turn as the breadwinner.

Donna enjoyed her new job, but it consumed her time and energy, just as running the business had consumed her husband's. Meanwhile, Bill now found himself immersed in the day-to-day household activities that for so long had been Donna's world. Each was experiencing life as the other had known it, and they would need some time for adjustment.

"Donna, look, I know you want this to turn out well," I told her, "but give him a chance. He's not doing it wrong. He's doing it his way, and that's okay. Let him figure it out. Pretty soon you might even find that he's running things better than ever."

She smiled faintly. "Well, I guess so," she said. "It just seems it would save us all a lot of trouble if he'd do what I say. He just has a mind of his own."

"That's the point!" I said. "He does! He's not you. Bill has his own ideas about the best way to do things. He wants the best for all of you. Try encouraging and empowering him instead of micromanaging him. He's not a child."

Donna looked thoughtful. As we parted, I suggested she wait

three months or so before drawing any conclusions. After all, wasn't she herself expecting to get at least that much time at her new job to prove herself?

As soon as Donna let go of trying to control her husband's responsibilities, the tensions between them eased. Bill learned through trial and error, discovered new approaches, and grew into his new role as the supporting man of the house.

SETTLING INTO
A NEW JOB

In a healthy relationship, the partners accept and appreciate each other's roles, but some couples sink into disrespect and disdain. The homemaker may come to believe that the breadwinner doesn't have a clue, and vice versa. Without a foundation of respect, the pillar of partnership will crumble.

I witnessed such disdain when I joined a parents' group in Munich after Dominik was born. We met twice a week for lunch or coffee, and usually, I was the only man among several women. I noticed that if one woman complained about how her husband handled tasks around the house, the others tended to chime in with their own stories of male incompetence, and the conversation would devolve into a roundtable session on what women have to tolerate from men.

After hearing such comments repeatedly, I offered my own perspective. "It's not that men can't do it, and it's not that they won't do it," I said. "It's that they haven't had much practice doing it. This has nothing to do with gender. I feel some of the same frustrations about how my wife does things as you do with your husbands. She's not incompetent, though. She is able. She just doesn't have the experience at running the household that I do. That's my job, not hers.

"Just imagine how you would feel," I continued, "if you took your husband's place at his job. On your first day, would you do everything as well as he does it? If you didn't have the training and experience, would you feel it fair to be ridiculed as incompetent?"

Couples should take care to empower each other, not undercut each other. Each, naturally, will do best at what he or she does daily, but that doesn't mean the other partner is in any way lacking. A loving breadwinner would never belittle the homemaker for lacking employment skills. Likewise, a loving homemaker should never belittle the breadwinner's shortcomings in domestic skills. Each could develop those skills if necessary. The couple, instead, should honor their mutual contributions to a thriving family.

It takes time to learn new skills, whether on the job or at home. A reasonable employer will give a newly hired worker some time, commonly a hundred days, as a learning period to adjust to the job. It takes at least that long to accurately assess whether the employee is a good fit for the position. On the first day, few people perform as a seasoned employee would. With the right tools and training, new hires will grow quickly if they have the ability, potential, and initiative.

EXPERIENCE IS A POWERFUL TEACHER. PEOPLE DON'T IMPROVE WHEN OTHERS DO THEIR WORK AND PICK UP THEIR MESS.

Experience is a powerful teacher. People don't improve when others do their work and pick up their mess. A frustrated supervisor who does an employee's job just to get it finished will end up even more frustrated. Excellence comes from trying, improvising, and trying again. Small successes lead to bigger ones. Missteps inspire firmer footing. If the supervisors constantly overrule and take over, they not only slow down the process of learning but also squelch individual initiative, particularly among the millennials who now dominate the workforce. The employees figure their contributions must not matter and stop trying to do a good job, eventually going elsewhere for job satisfaction.

Teachers and parents, at least the effective ones, know how to help young people develop a sense of independence and self-sufficiency. As much as teachers would like to provide all the answers, they watch their students struggle to come up with the answers. They know that students value knowledge more if they have worked hard to gain it, and their retention of it is better too. It would be easy for Mom and Dad to step in and solve problems big and small, but that would handicap kids more than help them.

Couples should embrace that wisdom. If the partners are redefining their roles in the family, they should anticipate a learning period and be careful not to get in the way of each other's progress. They should build each other up rather than tear each other down. Each partner should allow the other to have room for growth as, together, they adjust to the new roles they have chosen.

HANDING OVER THE KEYS

I met a couple who set themselves up for failure when they traded roles, and, again, a significant part of the problem was the attitude of the spouse who was returning to work. They thought they had it all planned out: as she pursued her career, he would take care of family matters. Except, not really. She didn't let him. She orchestrated the family schedules. She made the doctor appointments for their children. She chose their summer camps. His job was to fulfill and comply.

That poor husband was relegated to a position of little more than a chauffeur, following his wife's directives. He was not empowered to take charge of anything. He had less power in his family than the stay-at-home mom typically has in more traditional family models. His wife figured he wouldn't get it right, but it was she who was doing it wrong.

What was driving the wife to such extremes was her fundamental inability to redefine her personal definition of womanhood. Though in most respects she was a modern thinker, she felt deep within that it was her job to nurture the children, even though her career responsibilities left her short on time and energy for such a huge family responsibility. She was reluctant to hand over the keys to the kingdom.

Her husband could have stepped up to that challenge if she had entrusted him with real decision making authority. She preferred, instead, to use him as a functionary who would do her bidding so that she could hold on to her mom image. In effect, she reduced him to being her puppet. She may not have realized what she was doing, but he felt that way, and their children saw what was happening and felt less respect for him. They saw him more as a babysitter who reported to Mom than as a parent who would deal with them directly. It wasn't a healthy dynamic. This was a family at risk.

This sad scenario is repeated over and over in many families. As the woman heads out to build her career, she hands over the household tasks but not the responsibility for them. In trying to please her, the man jumps to do things her way and never gets on the learning curve. He loses the opportunity to make those missteps that will help him to excel as he improvises.

As a result, the man doesn't take much pride in what he does. Why should he learn more and strive to do better when his job description, basically, is that of errand boy? He feels he has been assigned a series of tasks and just wants to get them completed without much thought for how to do them better. He doesn't feel he has a personal stake in the outcome.[4]

Sometimes the wife makes matters even worse by questioning her husband's competence and character, insinuating that she can't trust him with such authority. She points to his inevitable missteps as evidence of her superiority. She communicates to him that she *must* because he *can't*. She then becomes convinced that he is not pulling his weight, and she presumes that he just doesn't care. Feeling that he is failing to support her needs, she loses respect for him.

In truth, he can handle these responsibilities without her oversight and micromanaging. and she simply can't do it all. She won't admit that to herself, though. She is rationalizing her own insecurities. She is trying to claim all the pride for herself and denying her husband his share.

I know a family in which the working wife plans the entire week's menu. Her husband simply shops for the food and ingredients and prepares them at the appointed time, cooking them to her specifications. That's not an equal partnership. That almost inevitably will generate tensions in the relationship.

In an equal partnership, the one who is entrusted with a family responsibility—whether it is bringing home a paycheck, making the meals, handling the finances, disciplining the children, and so on—

---

4   Alison Byrne and Julian Barling, "Does a Woman's High-Status Career Hurt Her Marriage? Not if Her Husband Does the Laundry," *Harvard Business Review*, May 2, 2017, https://hbr.org/2017/05/does-a-womans-high-status-career-hurt-her-marriage-not-if-her-husband-does-the-laundry.

must be free to do it as he or she feels is appropriate, so long as the results reasonably serve the family's best interests. The other partner must be willing to accept that approach. If one partner has been using spreadsheets to track finances, for example, but the other starts stuffing receipts and records into a shoebox, then so be it. If you get to the end of the month and the bills have been paid and the budget is in good shape, why fuss about how you got there? In our family, I choose which summer camps our children will attend. Mirka offers good suggestions, and I consider them carefully, but she feels no need to micromanage me.

Adjusting to new roles can take time. Egos and pride get in the way. The one who had brought home the paycheck might feel somehow less important in the new job of tending to the home and children. The former homemaker likewise can feel displaced. With patience and understanding, each should adjust well to the model that together they have agreed to adopt. After all, they are making this change because both have decided that it would be good for them and for the family. Nobody said it would be easy.

Loving partners bestow the gift of self-reliance generously on each other. They do for each other what good parents do, though their relationship is not paternal. They do for each other what good teachers do, though their relationship should not be one of instruction and direction. They do for each other what good supervisors do for their employees, though neither partner should presume to be the boss of the other. Each must be willing to step back, patiently and respectfully, to allow the other to build a sense of pride in a job well done.

There are many roads to Rome. Some are straight, some are winding, some are smooth, some have a few potholes to repair. But unless someone has put barricades in the way, all those roads lead to the same destination.

KEEPING
ON TRACK

To empower your partner, you must look beyond your own interests and carefully consider his or her needs and wants. You can't read each other's minds. The only way to find out about your partner's expectations is to talk regularly and thoroughly about your journey through life and listen carefully to what you hear. If necessary, you may need to reassess and adjust the family model that you have chosen. You may even need to define a new one. Though you are in this together, you still are individuals with your own ideas, desires, and dreams. Sacrificing does not mean losing yourself.

SACRIFICING DOES NOT MEAN LOSING YOURSELF.

I met a couple who found a way to accommodate and support each of their career ambitions without calling an end to their relationship. The classic power couple, they did not have children, and both were striving to be high achievers in their professions. As he was preparing to launch a company in England, she received an exciting offer to take over a position in Dubai. It was a major opportunity for her, but it conflicted with his plans since he would not be able to run his company from five thousand miles away.

The couple had to make a decision, and so together they weighed all their options and decided on a five-year plan. They moved to Dubai. After three years there, he returned to England to start his company. She remained in Dubai for an additional two years, and then they reunited in England. A five-year separation would have been quite a challenge to their relationship, but they felt that they could manage being apart for that final stretch. Until then he postponed his business plans, stepping back to support her and to help her realize her dreams.

Conflicts are common in any relationship, though most do not require such dramatic change. A lot of smaller conflicts, however, can add up to destructive tension. If a couple hope to stay together, they should look for a true solution that is neither selfish nor selfless. By talking and sharing their feelings, they can find a compromise that works for both of them without diminishing the dreams of either of them.

Good communication is key. Each partner should listen to the other with heartfelt attention, and they each should express clearly their own needs and wants. Even when the couple's roles and responsibilities are clearly defined, each partner should be free to weigh in on all important family decisions because each has a major stake in the outcome. They should make the big decisions as a team, considering what is in the best interests of both partners and the family, over time.

Change can be exciting and empowering, but it can become frustrating and divisive unless the couple remains sensitive to helping each other become their very best. If they see each other as equals and respect each other's roles, they will be eager to hear what each other has to say. Disagreement is healthy when it leads to better ideas. It leads to bickering only when the partners lack confidence in where they stand in the family. Insecure people try to silence dissent. Secure people welcome it.

Mirka often has told me that she believes we could do this or that differently. If she is referring to something that is my primary responsibility, she knows that I will respect and consider her views. If what she is telling me is a better idea, I am open to changing my approach. Likewise, she carefully considers my opinions about how her career choices will affect our family. We trust that we both are acting in the best interest of us all.

Though neither partner should micromanage the other's responsibilities, both should macromanage their mutual vision. Each will care about the other's actions and decisions. After all, they are in this together. They are planning their lives together, dreaming together. They can delegate the details, but when it comes to the big picture, they should feel free to speak their minds.

The time may come when the couple decide that their family model no longer works. One partner or the other may start to feel that the division of labor is unfair. For example, at the end of an exhausting day, the one who has been working outside the home for eight hours or more may begin to resent the duty of doing the dishes: Don't I do enough for this family without coming home to clean up a mess in the sink? Meanwhile, the one who tends to the household for twenty-four hours a day may also resent doing the dishes, and a lot of other things, as a sense of unrest wells up from the heart: When do I get my chance? Don't I matter, too?

Every family will establish its own standards and rules for what is fair. When it comes to housework, for example, those rules will depend on what works for everyone. I certainly don't resent doing the dishes, for example, but there was a time when I served our meals on paper plates to make the chore easier—except when Mirka was home and able to join us at the table. She prefers that we eat from our china plates, so she cleans up the kitchen when she is with us. We agreed that was fair. More important is what we serve on those plates. I agree to put nutritious food on the table whether Mirka is home or not. Both of us are content with the arrangement because it serves that higher purpose while also considering our individual likes and dislikes.

In a healthy relationship, feelings of discontent must be addressed, or they will fester. The partners should regularly reassess their family model, because it can change through the years. Sometimes they simply need to regain a healthy perspective on how much each truly is contributing. They may need to get back in touch with their dreams and renew their vision. Eventually, though, they may wish to pursue new dreams and a new vision, and if they are to do that together, one thing is certain: It's time to talk. If either partner is fundamentally unhappy, they can't let it slide.

IN A HEALTHY RELATIONSHIP, FEELINGS OF DISCONTENT MUST BE ADDRESSED, OR THEY WILL FESTER.

What matters most are the results. Is the couple making progress toward shared goals and dreams? If not, then it's time to revisit and fine-tune their role definitions and relationship. If something isn't working, it could get worse if left unaddressed. Even then, though, they should proceed with caution as they look for improvements in procedure.

The attitude should never be "See, your way is a failure, so we will do it my way." Instead, it should be more like this: "Help me understand your way so that perhaps I can offer ideas to help us work together even better." That's what strengthens a pillar of partnership. Respect and kindness go a long way toward bringing out the best in everyone.

Compassion, understanding, and acceptance are the ingredients for keeping a partnership on track for success. Both partners should take a deep breath and discuss matters calmly and dispassionately without interpreting disagreement as a challenge to their authority. They must show the resolve to handle their responsibilities as they feel best, and neither should jump through hoops just to please the other. Nor should either of them prescribe a solution when the other hasn't asked for one. In other words, partners should be loving, patient, strong, true to themselves, and humble. Those are the tools for empowerment.

CHAPTER 5

THE WORK-LIFE BLEND

SELF, PARTNERSHIP, FAMILY, WORKPLACE & SOCIETY PILLARS

We hear a lot these days about finding the right balance between work life and family life, but is there really anything to balance? More accurately, it's all just the blend of life. Working together, supportive partners can make the most of both. That's how they can have it all.

Every one of the pillars comes into play here: **self, partnership, family, workplace, and society.**

"How do you manage to have any kind of a life, with all the time you put into your career and with all the traveling around the world you have to do?" a college student asked Mirka at a recent speaking engagement in Germany. "How do you find the right balance between work and life?"

She explained that it's not a matter of balancing them, as if they were separate things that you somehow could weigh on a scale. Instead, you integrate them. Your work life and personal life flow together as one. The blend will change through the years, sometimes more career, sometimes more family—but you are always immersed in both.

"It isn't as if work ends and life begins when you finally leave the office for the day," Mirka told her audience. "You aren't living in two different worlds. It's one world, and you're looking to make the most of it. So I don't think of it as a work-life balance. I think of it as a work-life blend."

It's a fact of life for high-performing executives such as Mirka: Sometimes they have to take their work home with them, and sometimes they may have to deal with situations at home while they are at work. Her work responsibilities are constantly on her mind, in one way or another, whether she is in the office or in our living room. Her family also is constantly on her mind. She does not cease to be a mom and a wife when she steps out the door each morning, or in her case, because she travels so much, when she steps onto a plane. She is always striving to find just the right blend.

Some would say that she wants to "have it all": both career and family. That's not something that people ever seem to say about men. And every female executive who is also a mother has heard this question: So who's home taking care of the kids while you're so busy? A father doesn't hear questions like that. The presumption is that his wife is there for the kids, and for him, so that he can come and go at any time. Intended or not, the implication is that taking care of children is primarily the mother's responsibility. That persistent attitude contributes to curbing women's progress in the workplace. Mothers get fewer job opportunities and promotions. You would think that they would get more, considering how skillful moms become at multitasking and prioritizing.

Mirka does have it all because we have structured our family to make it possible. Having it all doesn't mean doing it all. I am there for her and the children. I am her pillar in the home, providing the support she needs so that she can be both a loving mother and a successful business executive. We do it through teamwork.

That's not to say she couldn't do it without a partner, as many women do, but even single moms need a support system if they expect to pursue a demanding career. Some have the luxury of flexible hours, or they can work from home or part-time, with skill sets that compensate them well. Still, they will need child care. They will need help around the house. They can either hire that help or lean on family and friends with whom they have built strong and long-standing relationships.

A work-life blend requires compromise. Mirka would love to spend more time with our children and me, but her duties as a corporate CEO limit those hours. Everyone, however, has the same number of hours in a day. Using them wisely requires thoughtful planning that focuses on what matters most. Mirka and I emphasize the quality of our family's time together. So, she enjoys the enduring memories that come from well-focused hours with her loved ones while still devoting the necessary time to the career that she also loves. In both her home and her office, she can excel, and that is the perfect blend for fulfillment and happiness.

NO NEED TO
BE SUPERWOMAN

A woman with a successful career wears three hats, at least, on her weekends at home. She likely will still need to spend several hours on job responsibilities. Meanwhile, she will want to attend to her family's needs, which will include some chores around the house and various errands. And she needs time for herself, to go running, perhaps, or meet with friends, or enjoy a hobby. Not even Superwoman could do all that.

Torn between the demands of work and home, she wants to be there for her family as a nurturer but may feel that she cannot do that from a distance. She does not always recognize that using her skills and talents to provide a good income and prosperous lifestyle for her family also nurtures her family. It's okay to be away. I often tell Mirka how much we value her for using her gifts to make our lives all the better.

Not everyone feels that way about women in the workplace. People tend to view a man who spends countless hours on the job as a good caretaker of his family, but when a woman focuses on her job, she is often considered to be lacking in such devotion even though women have been rising to prominence in the workplace for a long time. Old attitudes linger through generations.

As a result, a woman whose role is not that of a traditional homemaker and nurturer may harbor a sense of guilt. Consciously or not, she feels judged, as if all eyes were on her, as if people were whispering, "Why aren't you taking good care of your kids and family? They need you at home, so why aren't you there for them?" A better question might be whether her family is there for her, after her exhausting hours on the job, but that point somehow gets missed. And so she tries to make up for lost time. She comes home after a day away, or a week away, and tries to be everything to everyone.

As a rule, when a man comes home from a hard day's work, he doesn't do that. He helps with chores as necessary but doesn't try to assume the role of full-time homemaker as well as full-time bread-winner. He doesn't feel he must take off his tie and put on an apron. Trusting that the affairs of the household are in good hands, he can finally relax.

That doesn't mean he's unwilling to help around the house when his partner needs him. It doesn't mean that he is not a devoted dad if he isn't always the one who checks the homework and tucks the kids into bed. It means he accepts that these are not his primary areas of responsibility. He is not weighed down by guilt. He is not subject to society's judgment that he should be home, taking care of his family. After all, doesn't a man take care of his family by heading out to work? He is doing what society expects of him, and so he feels right with the world.

A female breadwinner, typically, has a harder time achieving that sense of equanimity. She doesn't really feel right with the world either on the job or at home. Something different seems to be expected of her—and she often expects it of herself, particularly if she grew up in a traditional household. At work, she takes on responsibilities that, for generations, were not part of the world of women. Yet, after work, in her home, which for so long *was* the world of women, she cannot escape the added stress of feeling that she should be taking care of business.

> **MANY WOMEN TODAY ARE GAINING THE CONFIDENCE TO BREAK THE GLASS CEILING IN THE WORKPLACE.**

Many women today are gaining the confidence to break the glass ceiling in the workplace. They could use more of that confidence in their home lives, as well. Why feel guilty about success? They are not neglecting their families. Rather, they are providing well for them and demonstrating to young women everywhere that they, too, can make the most of their talents.

To be both breadwinner and homemaker is to have two jobs. How could anyone hope to relax under those circumstances? Those who try to do it all risk letting something slip, and a feeling of failure just worsens the stress. As they advance in their careers, women need a support structure at home, which why men, increasingly, have been rising to that challenge, sharing fairly in the domestic responsibilities. Many have demanding jobs of their own, but, nevertheless, some are taking on that support role full-time.

Supportive men have their own challenges. A man who has assumed the support role in the home may feel a similar level of stress. He, too, typically feels that fingers are pointed at him. If he does not have a paying job, he may imagine that people are whispering that he should be out there making a living for his family—and, frankly, a lot of people do think that way. He himself may believe that, particularly if he was raised in a traditional family.

These are the realities that men and women often face when they swap traditional roles. They are doing what makes perfect sense for the security and advancement of the family, and they are making good use of their personal resources, and yet they still must deal with prevailing societal attitudes or the lingering sentiments within themselves of what a "real" family looks like. They know better, of course, but emotions so often can get in the way. Understanding these conflicts is the first step to overcoming them.

Let this be the message to all working women from the men who care about them: You can't do it all, and that's all right. I respect and value what you do and I respect you.

A TIME
TO TALK

I have a friend, a female executive, who had to lay off two people one Friday afternoon. She came home with a need to talk. In fact, her husband got an earful for the entire weekend. I have another friend, a male executive, who had to lay off fifty people. His wife did not even know about it until later.

When men come home from work, they tend to not want to talk about their day. They put up a wall between their work lives and their home lives, keeping them separate so that they can relax. This compartmentalization can be quite frustrating for the women in their lives, who generally feel more relaxed after they have talked things through.

After a challenging day in the workplace, women tend to come home, looking for a sounding board. They bring their work home with them, looking for a companion who will listen to their frustrations, their ideas, and their ambitions. By talking through their key priorities and challenges, they can finally let go of them and refocus on the family

On the other hand, there are some men who like to review their day in the workplace, and some women who would rather not. Either way, each partner must understand the other's fundamental nature and needs. If a man comes home without much to say, he should not feel obliged to engage in conversation about his day. If a woman comes home full of talk, a wise man sits down with her and hears her out for a while. He does not immediately try to steer the conversation away from what she needs to say.

Don't make the mistake, though, that I and, I am sure, countless other men have made. As the husband of a high-level executive who often comes home with a lot on her mind, I can attest from experience that the man's job is mostly to listen. Mirka isn't particularly looking for my advice. She doesn't need to hear me expound upon what I think she should do. She's not asking me to solve anything. Usually, she already has a pretty good idea of what she needs to do

What my wife wants is my compassion and understanding. She needs a sympathetic ear. As she talks, she is thinking out loud. She is working out how she feels and deciding for herself which actions she should take, if any. And that is as it should be, since she, not I, is the expert on those matters. She deserves the dignity of self-direction. When I listen attentively, ask a few brief questions, reflect on what she is saying, and nod understandingly, I am helping her find the clarity that she needs. I might share with her what I did, or didn't do, in situations similar to hers, but I do not counsel her or tell her that my solutions should be hers too. Instead, I listen and I may ask a few open-ended questions to help her direct her thoughts—or at least that is what I know I should do. I confess that it is not what I always do.

Likewise, the partner who has been watching over the house and kids since daybreak should have time to talk and vent, and the one arriving home from work should mostly just listen without offering unsolicited advice. That's not necessarily easy for a corporate leader who spends the day supervising and coaching others, but once he or she gets home, it's time to take off the boss hat.

Words such as the following are conversation stoppers: "You should do this," or "It's so simple, really," or "Has it occurred to you that …?" They communicate an arrogance that has no place in the relationship between equals. A compassionate listener will say things such as "Tell me more," or "How do you feel about that?" or "I understand." In an effort to uncover road blocks and underlying issues, he may also ask "Why?" This type of question tends to encourage communication and get to the heart of the matter.

Each partner should treat the other's heart with care and tenderness. They must be comfortable enough with each other to pour out their feelings and be vulnerable, without fear of judgment. They need to establish a safe haven for communication in which they can clear the air without risk to their relationship.

> **EACH PARTNER SHOULD TREAT THE OTHER'S HEART WITH CARE AND TENDERNESS.**

A certain amount of shop talk can be helpful, but too much is not. It's a balancing act. For most couples, it would be unwise to decree that there will be no shop talk at home. Better to limit the discussion, not suppress it. "Okay, let's hear about your day, even for an hour if you'd like," a loving spouse might say, "and we can talk more later if that is not enough, but let's also make sure that we spend some time just enjoying being with each other and the kids." Both partners need to feel that they have been heard, but not to the point of nonstop rehashing, which could wear them both out and worsen their stress rather than relieve it. This should be family time, quality time, when everyone has a chance to relax.

A TIME TO RELAX

Couples need to schedule time to relax, whether a date night, a weekend in a hotel, or a longer getaway. Many vacation spots offer couple retreats with facilities for connecting and relaxing. If you don't set aside that time to take care of yourselves and your relationship, you risk burning out. To take advantage of those opportunities, though, you have to plan for them, or they will not happen. You must set aside the time on your calendar,

A wide variety of resources are available for couples wanting to share more time together. A friend of mine, Kelly Clements, wrote a book on this subject titled *The Power of Play, Praise and Purpose: The Best Kept Secrets of Thriving Entrepreneurial Couples*. Though the book focuses on entrepreneurial couples, the lessons apply to any couple seeking to integrate home life and work life.

Harmony is the key. As a good manager, Mirka intimately understands the concept of delegation and clear lines of responsibility. She does not have to do it all, because she trusts that I will be there for our family in the support role. That is why she defers to my decisions regarding family affairs. She doesn't try to superimpose her own views, because she knows that, generally, I have things under control. She shows me that respect.

By taking care of the details of home life, I give her the freedom to relax. It's not unusual for a hard-working man to spend a Saturday afternoon on the couch drinking a beer and watching a football game. Why shouldn't a hard-working woman have such an opportunity to take a break? And yet if she comes home and spends time watching television or reading a book while her husband does the dishes and mows the grass, people might find that strange. Yet, she is doing what men have done for ages: accepting the support of a loving partner and feeling secure in that embrace. It is my privilege to be able to offer my wife that sort of support, and I feel fulfilled when she accepts it.

Not all women respond like that. Successful female executives tend to be highly responsible achievers who want to personally make things happen and see them to completion. They may be reluctant to take a break even when they can because they see so much around them that still could be done. They go back into executive mode. Sometimes they issue directives to their partner to take care of this or that, forgetting that he needs a break, too, and sometimes they try to deal with all those odds and ends themselves. It can be hard for them to switch out of accomplishment mode, but they must. Otherwise, they might run in circles until they drop from exhaustion.

To avoid burnout, women in high-stress careers should regularly include break time in their schedule along with everything else that they pack into it. It's all part of wise self-management. If either partner in a relationship is chronically exhausted, the whole family will be at risk of falling apart.

THE SANCTUARY OF HOME

One weekend when she was home with us, I could see in Mirka's eyes how proud she was of herself for being able to take Viktoria to a friend's birthday party, and Viktoria was thrilled to have this special time with her mom. At the party, while Viktoria was having fun with her playmates, Mirka sat down with several of the other mothers who were there. All of them seemed to be friends with one another. She didn't know any of them. How could she? But still, she tried to engage with them in small talk around the table.

"So who is your daughter's teacher? Is she in the same class with Mrs. Clark, as my Cindy?" one of the women asked her. Mirka didn't know either Mrs. Clark or Cindy.

"Have you started working with your daughter on her science

fair project?" another asked. She hadn't, of course, not because she didn't care but because that was my responsibility, and I am always a last-minute project doer.

Another of the women, perhaps hoping to help Mirka feel included in their circle, suggested that she might want to make cupcakes for their PTA meeting the following Friday. Mirka confessed that she could not do so, because, after all, she would be about four thousand miles away by then.

It went downhill from there. Mirka came home feeling deflated. She felt out of the loop. She was left wondering whether those women believed that she was not a good mom or a good wife. I reassured her that she was both. It didn't matter whether they understood that. I understood that. Our children understood that.

Such is life for successful women executives who come home from a demanding day and try to fit in. Their accomplishments often conflict with society's expectations, and with their own expectations. Old-school attitudes seem to conspire to drive them down. They need someone in their lives to build them up, to recharge them, to reassure them.

Mirka knows what needs to be done, both at work and at home. She has proven herself, over and over. As for me, I am devoted to serving our family. For now, this is what I need to do, and I have the privilege and opportunity to watch our children growing up, every day, all day. My job is to take good care of them so that they grow up happy—and to keep my wife happy as well so that she can keep on doing what she does so well. I ensure that our home is a sanctuary for her where she can renew her strength and confidence to go out and be all that she can be. Together we have found the right blend.

CHAPTER 6

FINDING STRENGTHS TOGETHER

SELF & PARTNERSHIP PILLARS

Developing a supportive relationship begins with getting to know yourself and understanding your unique set of strengths. Once you and your partner learn who you are as individuals, and how you fit in, you can work together to more efficiently define the appropriate roles for each of you. You each can maximize your talents, becoming the best possible version of yourselves and creating a powerful and fulfilling team.

The pillars of self and partnership are the focus of this journey of discovery.

When I think back to those days when Mirka and I fell in love, I still marvel that she married this man whose education, occupation, and sophistication were no match for hers. We traveled in different circles. In fact, unlike her, I hadn't traveled much at all. And yet she chose me over all the hotshots whose ambitions didn't include her happiness.

It wasn't that I was some loser who wouldn't get in her way. On the contrary, Mirka acknowledges that she married a man of strength. She didn't see weakness. She saw a man strong enough to overcome ego. Unlike the other men she had met, I applauded her career ambitions. I paid attention to more than myself. I supported what she needed and what we would need as a couple and as a family.

As we got to know each other, she recognized that my style of servant leadership would serve us well as we built a life together and a family. I am deliberative and analytical. In whatever I do, I ponder my decisions. I question each step. That quality should help anyone to lead a family, but it is not a prerequisite for success. It is simply me. Some see me as a perfectionist and prefer a more casual approach. A family can thrive under a variety of leadership styles. Mirka and I have found what works for us.

What works for nobody is a stubborn determination to hold on to an outdated way of thinking. The ego can get in the way. Some men, for example, cannot imagine themselves doing what I do. They see the household support role as the realm of women. A real man, they believe, is a breadwinner, not a housekeeper. He gets up each day to go to work, not to get the kids off to school. If those men set their mind to it, however, they could do it. There's not some mom gene that predisposes people to nurturing and supporting. It's not a matter of genetics. It's a matter of stepping up and doing what makes sense under the circumstances.

It is my nature to question the status quo. I am inclined to contemplate whether I am pursuing the best approach, weighing both the advantages and the risks. I am not satisfied with what is merely sufficient. Always on my mind are these questions: How can I do this better? How can we do it better together? Doing things in a certain way because they've always been done that way won't do, because that unquestioning attitude might just be the problem.

People bring a variety of strengths to a relationship. Some of those strengths are natural inclinations, and some have been developed through experience. Often, what might seem to be weaknesses are more like blind spots. You can't understand what you have yet to see. Ignorance is not a sign of poor character, just as a flabby muscle is not a sign of poor health. It is an opportunity for growth and development. You grow stronger when you exercise your body and when you exercise your mind.

YOU GROW STRONGER WHEN YOU EXERCISE YOUR BODY AND WHEN YOU EXERCISE YOUR MIND.

Your outlook on life has much to do with how willing you are to exercise your mind. Carol Dweck, a longtime psychology professor, most recently at Stanford University, developed the concept of the growth mindset by which people can attain great accomplishments with the right strategies and effort. The author of *Mindset: The New Psychology of Success* (2006), she has focused her research on motivation. Some people believe they are born with a set of talents that are fixed for life, while others believe they can develop themselves through hard work and determination. Those with a fixed mindset may fear failure as an indictment of their intelligence or lack of intelligence, while those with a growth mindset see failure as an opportunity to learn and develop.

Dweck's research suggests that people with a growth mindset experience less stress and more success in life. Despite setbacks, they keep working hard, anticipating that they will improve. Those with a fixed mindset are more likely to give up when they encounter a setback out of a concern that others will view them as not smart enough. Dweck's findings suggest that parents can help their children develop a growth mindset by praising them for their hard work when they do a good job rather than by telling them how smart they are.

A fixed mindset limits personal growth and development. In my youth, I was culturally limited. I grew up in a small town and didn't spend much time thinking about the broader world. Whatever I needed was within reach, I figured. My reach didn't extend far from my childhood home. That was my blind spot. It held me back. My horizon expanded when I met Mirka, and it changed even more when we moved to the United States to further her career.

Adjusting to this new way of thinking was not easy, but I considered it an adventure. I saw an opportunity to grow, to develop, to improve, to pursue better ways. I am open and adaptable to other perspectives and lifestyles. That is my inner strength. Nothing should be set in stone, including the roles of men and women in a relationship. My eyes opened wide to a world of possibilities, and I was able to see what Mirka saw in me.

ASSESSING ONE'S STRENGTHS

As a man who appreciates new and better ideas, I also recognize that these are often time-tested concepts that have simply been given new names, which holds true for the power of positivity over negativity.

Look on the bright side, every cloud has a silver lining, keep your chin up, count your blessings, you can do it, never say never—the truth feels trite when repeated incessantly, but it is still the truth. Positive thinking is an age-old prescription for success and prosperity.

It is also the focus of a primary tool, the CliftonStrengths assessment, which I am certified to use in my coaching business. It was developed by Donald O. Clifton, who was chairman of Gallup, Inc., and whom the American Psychological Association has recognized as the father of strengths-based psychology and the grandfather of positive psychology. The assessment identifies a person's unique sequence of thirty-four themes that make up personality and innate talents.

"What will happen when we think about what is right with people rather than fixating on what is wrong with them?" Clifton asked in the 1950s, when he was a professor of educational psychology at the University of Nebraska at Lincoln. In his two decades there, his research included studies on what distinguished talented people from others. Typically, he said, psychologists focus on the negative. Why not the positive? He wanted to learn how and why they excelled. In his quest for answers, he studied college tutors and others, concluding that successful people possess identifiable traits that benefit them in their careers.

After leaving the university in 1969, Clifton founded Selection Research Inc., offering services to help organizations choose the right employees for the right jobs. In 1988, his firm acquired Gallup, widely known for its public opinion polls. Under his leadership as chairman, the company expanded into a management consultancy specializing in how to make the most of employee strengths. In 1999, he established Clifton StrengthsFinder, the online tool now known as CliftonStrengths. It has since been used by many major companies, governmental agencies, the military, schools, and universities, as well as the World Bank and the United Nations. As I write this, twenty million people have taken the assessment.

The assessment is not just for organizational use. For a small fee, everybody can take the assessment online and discover their dominant talents and their blind spots. They can use the strengths-based approach not only in their careers but also in their relationships and in the leadership of their families. It's a valuable perspective for the workplace, school, and home. Why keep telling yourself what you think you can't do? Start telling yourself what you do well and can do better.

The CliftonStrengths approach advocates a diversity of personalities when building a team. Instead of assembling a group of people who are alike, why not look for people of different perspectives and strengths? By leveraging their differences, the team accomplishes more. That principle applies to a couple, too, who also must function as a team. They can accomplish more when they celebrate their differences.

RISING ABOVE NEGATIVITY

By learning what you naturally do best, you can focus on developing personal areas that have the most positive impact—and that doesn't mean concentrating on traits that have not surfaced as your strong points. Quite the opposite. The strengths-based approach does not emphasize the negative. It's all about the positive. The research indicates that people will improve only marginally when they spend their energies trying to develop talents they lack. When they pour that energy into developing their natural abilities, however, they can improve those traits exponentially.

A research study from the 1950s, for example, followed two groups of high school sophomores through the same speed-reading program.[5] In one group were students whose test scores before entering the program indicated that they already were relatively fast readers. In the other group were students of average ability. At the end of the program, the average readers' test scores increased somewhat. The scores of the gifted students, however, increased phenomenally, from an average of 300 words per minute at the outset to 2,900 words per minute by the end of the study.

The pursuit of excellence is a much better investment of your time and resources than a slight gain in mediocrity. Time isn't limitless. We need to make the best use of it by giving our best to the world, and by encouraging our loved ones to do the same. Let's say your child brings home a report card with a couple of As, a few Cs and a D. What draws your attention first? Do you praise the As, or do you zero in on the D or the Cs, railing and taking away privileges until those grades improve? Have you noticed where your child consistently gets those As? That tells you something about his or her natural strengths, even though a child's true talents might not bloom until later. What subjects does the child seem to most enjoy?

THE PURSUIT OF EXCELLENCE IS A MUCH BETTER INVESTMENT OF YOUR TIME AND RESOURCES THAN A SLIGHT GAIN IN MEDIOCRITY.

Sure, getting good grades all around is important—and the child may need a tutor—but by emphasizing the positive, you will

5   Donald O. Clifton and James K. Harter, "Investing in Strengths," *Positive Organizational Scholarship: Foundations of a New Discipline*, accessed August 6, 2019, http://media.gallup.com/documents/whitepaper--investinginstrengths.pdf.

be more likely to instill self-confidence and a love of learning. The same principle holds for athletics. Where does the child excel? Focus on that. A child whose heart isn't into a particular sport is unlikely to become an ace player. Whether you are a parent, a partner, an employer, or a coach, the lesson is clear. If you set your sights solely on what is wrong, you could crush the spirit. By focusing on strengths, you bring out the best.

PARTNERS
IN STRENGTH

Couples who take the strength-based approach to their relationship are more likely to focus on how each partner can support the other rather than fixating on the petty annoyances that could divide them. So many people squander their time and energies over trifles. Let's say your partner often leaves the cap off the toothpaste. You might mention it, certainly, if it matters that much to you, but harping will only hurt. Even if that habit were to change, how much have you gained? You lose more than you win.

Far better for couples to walk in gratitude, emphasizing what each partner contributes to strengthen their relationship and family. Mirka doesn't always do things exactly as I would like her to do them, nor do I meet all her expectations. In the big picture, though, I see how much she does for us, and her family's appreciation encourages her to do even more. It's a matter of balance: Couples who bicker about the small stuff have trouble seeing the big picture.

Negative thinking stifles growth. When you tell yourself you can't do something, you probably won't be able to do it. It becomes a self-fulfilling prophecy. When you tell yourself you can, you will likely find a way. And when the partners in a relationship tell themselves that together they can build a prosperous future, they will likely combine forces to accomplish more than they might ever have expected. Like a braided cord, they are stronger together than either could be alone.

The couples who succeed are those who learn to accept each other for who they are. Neither partner expects to change the other, but both plan to change together as they pursue great goals. They are clear about who will be handling which responsibilities, and each gives the other the freedom of discretion. The emphasis should not be on how the job is done but on whether it gets done. And neither partner should be keeping score of who slips up the most. They shouldn't be competing. They should be complementing.

You gain nothing by trying to force your partner to fit your mold. If you try to control, you will end up losing control. Instead, celebrate your differences and make the most of them. Mirka cannot change the meticulous way in which I reach decisions, and if she could, it would weaken us as a couple and as a family. Nor can I change her style of decision making and leadership. Even when I sometimes disagree with how she deals with an issue, I accept her nature. I value who she is. She doesn't have to prove herself. She has amply demonstrated her strengths to me, and I have demonstrated mine to her.

The results matter more than the process. What one partner considers a job well done, the other might consider a mess, and that is because they do not see life through the same lens. As individuals with unique strengths, they differ in their perspectives and priorities. Think of it this way: Two authors have written best-selling books. One works at a desk that is a jumble of papers, unopened mail, candy wrappers, and assorted junk stuffed into half-open drawers. The other works at a desk with a place for everything and everything in its place, lined up geometrically. The first you might call a slob, the other a neat freak. But why call them anything? After all, both wrote best-selling books.

That is the essence of the CliftonStrenths approach. We each can find our own way to excellence. The assessment is not designed to tell you which jobs would be a good fit for you. It is not meant to tell you whether you should be a plumber, or a writer, or a firefighter, or a business executive. Rather, it is designed to identify the natural talents that you could bring to any job, whether in the workplace or at home. Potentially, you could do most anything, but you would do it in your own way. Each of us is unique and possesses primary and secondary strengths unlike that of anyone else. Because I am deliberative, my approach to a given situation will differ from someone whose primary strength is harmony, for example, or command.

The circumstances will determine the right course of action for a couple, and if they are open to trying something different, they can find both career and family fulfillment. They might pull up stakes, for example, and cross the ocean to live in an unfamiliar country and culture. They might build a life together in which she pursues an illustrious career while he keeps the household in good order. If they work as a supportive team and pull together, confident in their roles, they can live a life of possibilities. They truly can be partners in strength.

PARENTS IN STRENGTH

Our children both participate in swim programs, but they look at swimming races in two quite different ways. A dominant strength for Dominik is competition. Viktoria adopts a futuristic outlook on life. To motivate our son, I tell him to look right and left at the two kids he's racing and kick their butts. That kind of pep talk would not inspire our daughter. She could not care less about competition. To motivate her, I appeal to her dreams and ambitions. "Honey, you will want to win this race to keep on track with becoming an Olympic gold medalist," I tell her.

I choose my words for both with the same goal of inspiring them to get to the other side of the pool as fast as possible. Their minds and hearts function differently, however, and so I must treat them differently. In the same way that partners can work better together when they understand what motivates each other, they can also parent much more effectively when they understand what motivates their kids.

CliftonStrengths offers a program designed especially for kids to help them discover and develop their talents. The assessment, for kids ages ten to fourteen, is called StrengthsExplorer. It identifies their top three talents, and the accompanying report suggests how they might best use them to learn and grow.

It's also a valuable tool to help teachers and counselors tailor their approach as they reach out to young people, all of whom are unique individuals. Children who discover their talents tend to show more confidence and resilience. They become more engaged in their school work and more interested in what the future holds for them.

> IN THE SAME WAY THAT PARTNERS CAN WORK BETTER TOGETHER WHEN THEY UNDERSTAND WHAT MOTIVATES EACH OTHER, THEY CAN ALSO PARENT MUCH MORE EFFECTIVELY WHEN THEY UNDERSTAND WHAT MOTIVATES THEIR KIDS.

BEWARE THE EDUCATION GAP

Have you ever looked around you at your fellow diners in a restaurant? Over there, in the corner, a couple are engaged in an animated conversation as if they were newlyweds. They delight in sharing ideas and perspectives and observations. Meanwhile, at another table, a couple stare glumly into the candle, waiting for their server. It seems that whatever they might have had to talk about, they finished that conversation years ago.

As couples develop their individual strengths, they must take care that they do not drift so far apart in their understanding of each other that their relationship suffers. To avoid that, they need to take an active interest in what the other is doing so that they can carry on a meaningful conversation. Otherwise, they may wonder what happened to that person they had been attracted to twenty years previously.

The education gap often develops when one partner gets management training at work and comes home bubbling with ideas and wanting to talk about them. As that partner learns more and more, the other doesn't keep up. He or she may have been more interested in learning about how to efficiently run a household, or about childhood education. Neither pursuit is superior. They are simply different.

Unless both partners are open to hearing about each other's interests, they may find they're no longer able to connect. They will grow apart—or rather, they will not grow together. Each will be evolving in his or her own way.

The solution to promote togetherness is not complicated, and it starts with awareness of that risk. Go outside your comfort zone.

Attend a few keynote speeches or a workshop together so you have something to discuss. Listen to a TED talk or read a book that your partner recommends so that you are on the same page. You will not likely attain the same level of expertise, but you will be able to engage in an enlightened conversation. If your interactions stagnate, you or your partner could be tempted to look elsewhere for intellectual stimulation, and if you go there, your relationship will go nowhere.

Sharing is a big part of caring. If you and your partner hope to stay together, do not allow an education gap to come between you. If you put in the effort, you will see that it pays big dividends. It's all part of honoring each other's differences and finding strength in them.

GENERATIONS TOGETHER

Dominik recently attended a summer camp in Canada, operated by Me to We, an organization that inspires campers to take action on issues they are passionate about. The kids not only enjoy time around the campfire but also learn about leadership and team building to make a difference in the world.

Before Dominik left on that adventure, I got a call from a representative of the organization, asking a few additional questions, one of which was this: "We see that you have registered a boy to attend our summer camp. Is that the gender he is going by?"

I was pleasantly surprised. They cared about whether he identified as male or female. So I went to the source. "Dominik, they are asking whether you think of yourself as a boy or a girl."

"As a boy," he replied, and I relayed the information to the caller. Dominik was not offended. Nor was I. In fact, it was refreshing to encounter such a progressive attitude. Me to We is true to its principle of encouraging everyone to be themselves.

We each have our own style, and when we embrace our differences we can accomplish much more together. Just as individuals must understand how they are unique, we must also recognize and appreciate the unique contributions of people who are not like us. In our workplaces and in our homes, we must welcome people who have discovered a different way. If we put up walls to keep them away, we lose an opportunity to gain perspectives that would enrich us all. Together we are stronger.

The millennial generation, born between the 1980s and the mid-1990s, represents an ever-increasing proportion of today's workforce. On the whole, their attitudes, lifestyles and career considerations differ from their parents' choices for an array of reasons that have much to do with what they experienced while growing up. Each generation evolves from the previous one, reacting and building upon both the good and the bad.

EACH GENERATION EVOLVES FROM THE PREVIOUS ONE, REACTING AND BUILDING UPON BOTH THE GOOD AND THE BAD.

The millennials, who were born during the rise of the Internet and came of age in the era of social media, are a technologically connected bunch who are eager for the experiences the world has to offer. A sense of ethics and purpose drives them to pursue careers in which they can feel authentic and socially responsible. They want to do something that matters to them, and they seek frequent feedback on how they are performing on the job.

If the generations are to work together effectively, they need to accept one another's differences without judgment and view them as an asset. Employers who see the strength of the millennial mindset don't try to mold them into something else. Instead, they celebrate the strength of another way of thinking. That's what couples should do as they work together, and that's what the different generations should embrace.

Having grown up in a world of increasing diversity, millennials, as a group, are comfortable with it. They are oriented toward inclusion and tend to be open to the ways of other cultures. They accept those differences as strengths, much as partners in a healthy relationship build on each other's talents.

The millennials also tend to be more accepting of alternative lifestyles, and they are more likely to establish nontraditional households. In their world, it is normal for both partners to enjoy exciting careers while also raising a family, or for a man to take the lead in running the household while supporting the woman as she focuses on her work.

As the millennials get older and increasingly take leadership positions in workplaces and homes, it is likely that the old attitudes will continue to fade. What today we still call nontraditional will become the new norm, over time. The day will come when no one will think it unusual for a man to be home in the support role while his partner takes her rightful place in the upper ranks of corporate power. The day will come when, together, we find our strength.

GETTING STARTED ON THE JOURNEY

When I visit companies to propose conducting a CliftonStrengths workshop, I often encounter resistance from the more traditional generation. "We don't need a self-improvement course here," a gray-haired manager will say. "Hard work is the only thing we need."

Those who do seem receptive will generally ask why they should choose CliftonStrengths over other widely known assessments. They want to know how the Gallup program compares to, say, the Myers-Briggs Type Indicator or the DISC Profile.

The CliftonStrengths assessment focuses on identifying key talents that anyone can bring to any job, emphasizing strength over weakness, the positive over the negative. By helping you to get better acquainted with yourself, it can open your eyes so that you can become not only a better colleague in the workplace but also a better partner in your home life as together you align your strengths to best serve your family.

However, it is just one among a variety of such tools that are designed to foster a deeper understanding of how we can work more productively and live in harmony. As you consider where you want to go in life and how to track your goals, you can also consult a variety of other resources, such as Becoming Your Best (https://www.becomingyourbest.com/). Whatever tool you choose, start somewhere on that journey. The more that individuals learn about themselves, and the more that managers can learn about their employees and their generational differences, the better they will be able to work together.

These tools can help no matter which model you choose for your family. You might be a power couple, each pursuing a high-energy career. You might be a late bloomer who is entering the work force, or expecting to do so, after years spent raising the children. You might be a woman in the prime of an exciting but stressful career whose partner at home provides the family support that makes your ambitions possible. You might be a man in the traditional role of breadwinner, with a supportive mate at home. In any of those roles, a personality assessment will help you to gain clarity and become more intentional with your choices.

Each of those relationships involves some degree of sacrifice. If you are a mom whose career requires extensive travel, for example, you will see less of your kids. If you are a husband in a support role, you most likely will earn less money than your wife does. So, put aside your ego and accept your chosen role. Mean what you say. If you commit to supporting your partner in whatever role, then do it, and do it your way, using your unique combination of strengths.

If you agree to postpone your personal goals, you should understand clearly why you are doing so. You should be acting from a position of strength, not of resignation. It should be something you are eager to do for good reason, not a situation into which you fall by default. Instead of experiencing that sinking feeling that you are losing yourself, you will feel that you are rising to the challenge. When you recognize your personal strengths, and when you have a plan to use them both now and later to reach your goals, you will feel empowered. You will know that your time will come.

Personality assessments such as CliftonStrengths are designed to help us learn to do better and reach our full potential as a partner, parent, employee, and friend. Knowledge is power. Knowledge of yourself can change your destiny.

CHAPTER 7

WHAT ABOUT
THE KIDS?

FAMILY, PARTNERSHIP
& SOCIETY PILLARS

Couples who have children will understandably put a premium on developing their impressionable hearts and minds. As Mom and Dad go through their own difficult adjustments, they can be sure that the kids have a lot on their minds too. They will be looking for guidance from parents who show them love and care.

*This chapter focuses on the **pillar of family**. Also playing key roles are the **pillars of partnership and society**.*

One Friday afternoon, as we excitedly awaited Mirka's arrival home from a long business trip, our son turned down an invitation to visit a playmate over the weekend. "I can't," Dominik explained to him. "My mom's going to be home, and I want to spend time with her."

His friend could not understand. "What do you mean? Moms are always around. Don't you see her every day?" I know that both our children have experienced their share of such moments. "Don't you have a mom?" some of their other friends have asked when they see only me making the meals and picking them up at school. Dominik and Viktoria are quick to point out that they do have a mom and that she loves them very much.

A few weeks later, Dominik finally told me what had been happening. Some of his playmates had been giving him a hard time, implying that he was a mama's boy who preferred her over them. I talked to the other parents and helped him set the record straight with his friends by explaining our family model.

I am not a professional educator or child psychologist. I am just a loving dad who listens to his kids, and I am happy to offer my opinions and views here. Parents can help one another by sharing how they handle situations.

AS THE CHILDREN SEE IT

Even as parents deal with such frustrations while adjusting to the new norm, their children may be having a difficult time with their own adjustments. If Mom and Dad can negotiate a nontraditional arrangement and find ways to make it work, you would think that it would work well for the kids too. And it very well might—until they start talking with their friends.

Many of their friends will live in traditional households where Mom is home with them while Dad heads out to work each day. That is the world that many children know and understand, and when they see something that seems out of the ordinary to them, they will be quick to say, "So what's up with *that?*" Children are not the most tactful of creatures.

Like everyone else, children tend to seek acceptance. They care very much about what their peers think of them. They don't want to feel different. So, when their friends start to question their family situation, or even tease them about it, they need to be reassured that they are not misfits.

Children tend to see their lives in black and white. They are either normal, or they are not. They fit in, or they don't. In a non-traditional family, the adults are acutely aware that their approach might not be considered normal by others, but they move forward believing that they are making the right choice for themselves and their family. Their children, however, never had a say in the matter. Their norm is the life they experience, the one that their parents designed for them. The adults therefore are tasked with standing by their convictions and assuring the kids that they are all right.

Dominik and Viktoria are not alone among children trying to understand who they are and where they stand in a changing world. Kids of other cultures who find themselves in a foreign land battling a different culture can have a particularly hard time adjusting. Children whose parents have divorced may also feel the sting of feeling different. And a child whose parents are gay or lesbian may be taunted for having two dads, or two moms. It starts with "That's just weird!" It soon can become "You're a freak!"

Such cruelty should never be tolerated, but the adults sometimes fail to prepare the kids to deal with it. It may not occur to them to explain how they have structured the family and why. Children don't need to know everything, but they

CHILDREN DON'T NEED TO KNOW EVERYTHING, BUT THEY DO NEED TO KNOW SOMETHING. do need to know something. If they don't get it from their family, they will get it somewhere else, or they will guess—and they probably will get it wrong.

Viktoria and Dominik show an openness toward all people that I believe stems from their own experiences in our nontraditional family. One of their friends was growing up in a small California community with two moms until the couple divorced. That boy's life got complicated on a couple of levels—gay parents, divorced parents, small-town gossip—but when he was hanging out with our children, he felt comfortable and accepted. Children in such situations need an abundance of reassurance that they belong, that they are loved no matter what, and that nothing is strange about them or their families.

Viktoria regularly introduces us to her new friends from a variety of cultures—India, China, and Korea, for example. She and her brother instinctively reach out to help others feel accepted and included. They deliberately cultivate relationships with those who, for whatever reason, do not quite match the pattern. I have observed that children from nontraditional families tend to develop the sort of compassion and empathy that our world so badly needs. They might struggle with their own identities for a time as they look for ways to fit in, but they emerge with an appreciation for the spectrum of human diversity.

A CULTURE OF CARING

Children know when the grown-ups really care. What they want, above all, are parents who will give them heartfelt attention, who will look out for their best interests and clearly include them in their world. Kids thrive on love. Parents come in many shapes, sizes, and personalities, but if they don't show love for their children, they are not really parents at all.

My parenting style is not soft and coddling. I am down to earth with our children and feel that I can help them best by helping less. I will not carry my children's backpacks to the bus stop, for example. If they forget a water bottle or something, I will not run back to retrieve it. I have seen moms make a big fuss over a bump or a scraped knee, which of course elicits even more tears and wailing. My approach is to brush it off and move on. Children will test boundaries and cry over nothing if it brings them attention and a smothering of hugs. For the right reasons, they should get attention aplenty, of course, but I take care not to overdo it. If a child learns to manipulate, the habit can last a lifetime.

We are proud of our children's self-sufficiency. When Dominik was only six years old, we put him on a flight from Denver to Munich, by way of Frankfurt, to visit his grandparents. The good people at Lufthansa helped him, of course, but we trusted him to make that twenty-four-hour trip without us. Today, even when we are with him on a plane, he likes to sit apart from us to demonstrate his independent spirit. He and his sister do their own laundry and all the dishes. Every school day, since the first grade, they have been preparing and packing their own lunches. They can see themselves off to the school bus even if I don't get out of bed.

That does not make me an uncaring parent. That makes me a devoted dad who has given his kids the gift of self-reliance. It's good, of course, to be an advocate for your kids, so long as you are not crippling them. Sometimes parents become overprotective or overdirective, believing that they are equipping their children for life. In truth, they are doing the opposite. They want their children to have a wealth of experience but are denying them the experience of overcoming their own mistakes. They are sheltering them from the ways of the world. When the tough times come, as they invariably do, these young people will not have much practice in applying life's lessons.

I'm not saying that you shouldn't be warm and nurturing. I am saying that you should teach children to be self-reliant, independent, and tough too, but that tends to be a dad's parenting style. It's another face of love. Neither men nor women are naturally better at parenting. They just tend to be different, and as with so much else, our differences can make us stronger.

In some families, though, a sense of guilt can get in the way of good parenting. It happens often when the parents divorce, and one or the other, or both, tries to win the children over by catering to their every whim. It can happen, as well, when a busy parent cannot spend as much time with the children as he or she would like, due to career obligations. With so little time to spare, parents in that situation may fail to be strict when the child is testing the boundaries and needs discipline.

Children thrive in a culture of caring, where they have the freedom to be themselves. That does not mean, however, that anything goes. Tolerance of misbehavior does the child no favor. A loving parent enforces the rules consistently, and children respect that. They might never say so, but they do, even when they test the limits. Deep inside, kids feel secure when the grown-ups in their life have the confidence to show them right from wrong.

Children do best when they feel they are active participants in the family's plans. When appropriate, parents should include the children in those discussions so that they can observe how decisions are made in the family. It is another opportunity for parents to show by example how to work cooperatively and effectively. By paying attention to what their children have to say, they will be teaching them to listen attentively to others.

MR. MOM PROBLEMS

"Stay on the trail, boys," I reminded a group of four first-graders, including my son, during a school field trip for which I had volunteered as a chaperone. Perhaps it was my German accent, or my masculine voice, but somehow, two of the boys decided that I was mean, and they told their teacher. There was much crying involved.

The next day I was summoned to the school. "I hear that you were barking at our children," the teacher said. I assured her that I had talked to the boys in my normal tone, firm but not at all nasty, and that I simply had told them that they must follow the very rules that she herself had emphasized. After all, we're the adults in their lives. Aren't we supposed to be teaching young people to stay on the right path?

"Well, in any case," she said, "I think it will be better for everyone if you don't volunteer as a chaperone here anymore."

We so often hear that "it takes a village to raise a child." In that brief conversation, I felt banished from the village. For generations, the early school years were largely the dominion of women, and I still was viewed as an outsider. As a man running his household and taking care of his children, I was perceived to be out of place in that community—and, apparently, out of line.

Many men have experienced awkward moments as they step up to fill the support role for women rising high in their careers. They still often feel that they are viewed as an oddity and dismissed as a Mr. Mom, not to be taken seriously. Sometimes male caretakers encounter outright discrimination and suspicion. On several occasions, when our kids were younger and I took them to the playground, people came up to me as I sat on a bench and questioned why I was there. "Do you have a child with you who is using this playground?" What they really wanted to know was why this man was sitting alone watching children play. To them, I didn't fit in. I was an outsider, maybe even a threat.

I understand the concerns of a protective parent, of course, yet I still felt saddened to be singled out as if I had to justify my existence. No one would have questioned a woman sitting on that bench. She would never have felt that all eyes were on her every move.

She no doubt would understand how that feels, though. Women have often felt that they needed to justify their presence in the workplace, which for generations was largely a community of men. A woman entering their world was an outsider, maybe even a threat.

I look forward to the day when people will want only to fill a role with the best person for the job. I look forward to the day when all eyes will be on performance, not on the gender of the performer. I would like to think that day will come in my lifetime. I hope it comes in our children's lifetime.

EQUIPPED WITH CONFIDENCE

Confidence is born of positive experience. Success will send it soaring. You can't know what you can do, however, without testing your abilities, and that test can be as simple as a road trip.

Traditional families tend to plan their vacations around the weeks that the husband is off from work so that they can all travel together as a package. Generally, Mom plans the itinerary, and Dad takes the driver's seat once the family is under way, which is fine—when it works.

In our family, we have found something else that works, and it seems to be the pattern among other families like ours in which the breadwinner is a busy executive who often travels miles away from home.

I do most of the vacation planning for our family because I am confident that I can do it well. I try to include Mirka in those plans as much as possible, but she often has work responsibilities that conflict with the scheduling. She doesn't want those conflicts to hold back the children and me, and so we compromise. Whether we are going camping or touring a new locale, she joins us when she can to share a joyous weekend with her family before flying off again. Or sometimes the kids and I fly to wherever she is working if she can get away for a while. Our children understand that it is their mother's hard work and loving sacrifice that allow us such a luxury. Though we might share only half a vacation with her, without her there wouldn't be a vacation at all.

The traditional vacation planning model is often based on what the parents themselves experienced as they were growing up. They expect that the whole family will be able to arrange the same time off, and that the man will do the navigating while the woman does the nurturing. Unless they can follow that model, it doesn't feel like a vacation to them.

Even though Mirka and I grew up quite differently, we nonetheless have adjusted to circumstances. We have agreed on what works best for our family. We look forward to her joining us when she can. That is the expectation our family has adopted. We have met halfway. The right way to plan a vacation is what is right for the family.

A traditional family might not try a different approach to vacationing, because neither partner feels able to handle all the vacation responsibilities alone. Since the family has never vacationed with only one of the parents, the parents presume that it can't be managed that way. To that I say why not? Give it a try, and you likely will be surprised at what you can accomplish. Mirka and I know what we can do because we have both done it. We did what we needed to do, and we found that we were good at it.

IT'S TIME TO MOVE BEYOND THAT ANTIQUATED NOTION THAT MEN CAN'T DO THIS, OR WOMEN CAN'T DO THAT.

It's time to move beyond that antiquated notion that men can't do this, or women can't do that. They are able to do whatever they set their mind on achieving. Women can rise to the top of their careers. Men can do housework and take care of children. Once they see that they can do it, those doubts will fade away.

To that end, parents should take every opportunity to teach children to overcome gender stereotypes, and various advocacy groups have been established for that purpose. One notable organization is Girls Who Code (https://girlswhocode.com/), which offers programs seeking to build a pipeline of future female engineers and "to close the gender gap in technology and to change the image of what a programmer looks like and does." Another group is Strong Women, Strong Girls (https://swsg.org/), a mentorship organization that empowers girls from underserved neighborhoods to imagine a broader future" by surrounding them with a community of strong women role models from academia and the professions.

Meanwhile, as boys get used to brisk competition from strong girls, they will discard the notion of "the weaker sex" and learn to expect and appreciate women's powerful leadership roles in the working world. The boys, too, need inspiring role models. They need to observe real men who show by example that it is cool to support women—and not just with a paycheck.

As the adults in the household build confidence in themselves, the children likewise will gain their own confidence. They will see that their parents know what they are doing after all and that they are doing it quite well. They will see that the grown-ups have managed to set up a successful family, and when the kids grow up, they will have no misgivings about doing it the same way if they so desire.

THE ART OF LISTENING

Effective parents communicate freely and clearly. When the children come to Mom or Dad with questions, they seek assurance that they are safe and loved and that all is well in their household, no matter what other kids might insinuate. At an appropriate level, you should inform them about what is going on around them and what is in the works for the family—an upcoming move, for example, or a major purchase, or a vacation, or a long business trip. And if their family structure differs from that of most of their peers, or if it suddenly changes, they need to know why. The unknown can be frightening. The children whose parents ignore or dismiss their questions will believe something must be wrong. If they are constantly told to stay out of grown-up matters, they very well might cease asking the questions parents might not want to hear but should hear. They also will bury their feelings.

When the children feel they are active participants in the family's planning and know that someone cares enough to listen to them, their confidence will deepen. As they observe who decides what, and how, they will better understand their family model and their place in it. They will gain that sense of belonging that is crucial to a child's happiness.

One of the ways that Mirka and I involve our children in planning for our family is to encourage them to participate in our vacation planning, or in choosing their summer camps, or even in the weekly meal planning. We also let them know in advance when we anticipate big changes, such as the need to move, that will influence their lives. They do not just wake up one day to find their world reordered. They have a chance to tell us how they feel about things.

When you truly give children that opportunity, you strengthen your bond with them. Good communication does not come about automatically. It should be thoughtful and purposeful. You should ask specific questions and listen attentively.

"So what did you do in school today?" many parents ask half-heartedly, scarcely looking up as Johnny comes through the door.

"Nothing. The Martians came and vaporized everything with their laser ray."

"That's great, dear. Any homework?"

"Nope," he says, tossing his backpack on the couch as he heads to his room to play a video game (and vaporize aliens, presumably).

Generally, children will respond to meaningless questions with equally meaningless answers or even grunts, but they will pour out their hearts to a parent who shows a real interest in them. Imagine this conversation:

"How was math class? Did you get a chance to ask that question about multiplying fractions?"

"Yes, but the teacher gave us a bunch more of them to do. They are even harder, and I think I'm still doing something wrong. I'm worried about keeping up."

"We'll take a look later. I remember being confused about fractions too."

It doesn't matter whether you can figure out the fractions. Look at the whole picture. It's not just about how smart you are. It's about how caring you are. That's what makes you the hero. When you truly listen to your children, you will be teaching them to truly listen to others. Instead of grunting through life, they are more likely to develop into compassionate individuals who show a sincere interest in the world and the people around them.

TOOLS FOR CONNECTION

To help advance family communication, particularly with the children, here are some useful tools that you may wish to try out.

CONVERSATION CARDS

In the spirit of getting conversations started, many organizations use icebreakers for their business meetings or coaching sessions. Conversation cards are very effective and fun conversation starters. You have a pile of cards with questions on them. You take turns drawing a card and responding. It's mostly talking and listening. The strategy is to open up to others, and to pay attention as they open up to you. They are the types of question that can be effective icebreakers at networking events. In our family, we like to pull out those cards when we have dinner guests or holiday visitors. I also have my own set of question cards that I use in counseling sessions.

Here is a sampling of questions:

- If you could have one superpower, what would it be, and why?

- What's the hardest part about going to school/work?

- Pick three words to describe this past year.

- What's your favorite family tradition?

- Who is one person you admire and why do you admire that person?

A few of those questions are just for fun, but others dive deep to uncover feelings about relationships, goals, influences, struggles and successes, family dynamics, and more. Many of them are good questions for colleagues in the workplace to ask themselves as they sort through the busyness and get down to business. They are good questions for partners who seek a deeper understanding of each other. And they can be good questions for children, too, particularly if they are given their choice of two or three to answer. That way they do not feel put on the spot but still can talk about what is really on their mind. If they don't understand some of the questions, that's okay. Even if they start goofing around, maybe that's okay too, because they are spending time with Mom and Dad talking about some of the most important things in life.

VIDEO CALLING

A parent who travels a lot on business often wonders how to best keep in touch with the children back home. It can be difficult, particularly when a trip involves time zones that are hours apart. You can't just decide to call home from London when you finally have a moment, at 7 p.m. for example, because the kids back in Philadelphia would still be in school. If you try to be spontaneous, you are likely to get no answer. Those calls must be scheduled thoughtfully for a time that works at both ends.

Video calling has come a long way over the past several years, and thanks to technological advances, it has become easier for parents and children to stay in contact daily, even when they are thousands of miles apart. When Mirka is traveling, Viktoria plays the piano to her over the video call so her mom can hear her practicing.

During Dominik's last swim state championship, Mirka was out of town, but I dialed her in, live, so she could be part of the races in real time. It made us all feel a little closer. Viktoria has even tried to play board and card games with Mirka via video. Memory or Battleship work well on those calls.

With the advent of video calling, you at least can see each other's faces as you chat, and technological advances have made it easier than ever to make that connection. You still must plan those calls carefully to account for the time zones, but you can almost feel as if you are together in the same room. That makes the experience much more satisfying for both parent and child. Technology continues to shrink the distances.

DOUBLE JOURNALING

We know a family that keeps two journals: one at home, in which the kids write, and the other with Mom, as she travels. When Mom comes home, they switch journals. The children can read what she has written, and vice versa, before they each add more entries.

In effect, the trading of journals allows parent and child to share their experiences through the power of the written word. Each is keeping what amounts to a personal diary that the other is free to peruse. It's a diary that has no lock. It accomplishes more than recounting the events of the day, which is what tends to happen in a phone or video call between parent and child. Those are important, of course, but the journaling adds the big-picture perspectives and feelings that arise during their time apart. It's another form of connection.

A BUSINESS TRIP TOGETHER

Bringing your kids to work for a day is a fantastic way for the kids to get an idea of what the parents are doing at work. But how about stepping it up a notch and bringing your kids on a business trip?

Take the mystery out of what Mom or Dad does during business trips. How is all that time away spent? No amount of explaining can create as clear a picture as taking your son or daughter along on one of those trips. Choose one that presents an opportunity to observe a sampling of what you do—a visit to a customer's factory, perhaps, or to an evening trade show.

The child, of course, must be sufficiently mature to spend time alone while you are attending to your obligations, and that is part of the experience. While you are busy, your child will be sitting outside the conference room catching up on homework. Those trips aren't a vacation. They aren't about having fun. This is work. It can be stressful. It can be boring. The trip shows children that they aren't being forced to stay home with Mom or Dad while the other parent is romping on the beach.

Yes, your son or daughter should feel your enthusiasm and dedication for what you do—this is a great opportunity to instill a healthy work ethic and attitude—but it is also good to demonstrate that any job, in any career, includes routine moments that are less than exciting. Such is work, and such is life, and those who succeed in either must learn to accept that. If you arrange such a trip in the right spirit, your child will feel honored to be included in a part of your world that had seemed mysterious. A trip together helps to take away that mystery.

FAMILY MASTERMIND

The concept of mastermind groups is nothing new. Business organizations have been using this tool under various names, such as power groups, for many years. There are many different structures, but they all have this in common: a group of people meets under a certain set of rules and structure to build deep and meaningful relationships. What better place for a mastermind group than the family?

Here's how we do it. We meet once a month, without phones or other distractions. We start with an icebreaker, possibly a few rounds of the conversation cards. Then we do an update, in which each of us answers the same questions, taking three to five minutes—for example,

What was the best thing that happened in the last month? What was the most challenging? What are you most looking forward to during the next month? What challenge will you face in the next month?

Every family can come up with its own set of questions. Of key importance is expressing feelings. This should not simply be a recounting of situations and events. Instead, we emphasize why our experiences were important and how we felt about them. After the update, we spend time talking about one important topic, which could come either from a list prepared in advance or from something that came up during the update. It might involve a problem that needs to be solved, family plans, or anything else that is meaningful. Through it all, we remain respectful and open to one another. Our goal here is to share experiences, not to give advice.

A LEGACY OF HARMONY

Throughout this book, you see example after example of how parents interrelate with their kids. Whenever there are little ones in the household, their interests rise to become high priorities. Good parenting starts with a couple's understanding of each other and their mutual needs. Their successful communication with one another is essential if they are to establish an effective household structure, a game plan for their lives together. What they do for themselves, they do for their children.

People often have asked me if I can suggest something more specific. How can they help their children to feel more comfortable as they cope with a lifestyle that may be much different from that of many of their friends? Some of those who ask that question are women executives whose husbands are running the household. Others are single moms, perhaps divorced or widowed, who are trying to develop their careers. Others are single dads who, likewise, are doing it all themselves. The same questions hold for couples who work while trying to raise a family: What about the kids? What tools can parents use to build stronger family bonds?

In this chapter I have shared a few of the tools that have worked for my family or for the families of friends. I am confident they will help your family, too, as you take the right steps to help your children deal with the differences among us. This is no small matter. Those kids will go on to establish their own families, and they will bring with them the life skills and the attitudes that they learned along the way. Caring parents do whatever they can for the generations to come to live in harmony with others. That should be our legacy, and it all starts with what we do today.

CHAPTER 8

WORKING TO MAKE IT WORK

WORKPLACE, SELF
& PARTNERSHIP PILLARS

Work issues are a central consideration as women rise in leadership and men step forward to support those ambitions. Women have long faced a range of workplace issues, including discrimination and harassment and unequal pay. And as men increasingly offer their support, they, too, face a range of work-related issues.

*The **workplace pillar** is front and center in this chapter. We also consider the interplay of **the pillars of self and partnership.***

The story of Mirka and me is one that many will recognize as women advance in their careers: adapting to the realities of life, making the best use of individual strengths, and building a future. It is a story of both partners working together to make a happy and successful life for themselves.

I grew up in Germany, near Augsburg. My family was traditional in the sense that my father worked full-time and made the major household decisions. However, my mother worked too. Her family operated a grocery store where she had helped since childhood, so I grew up seeing both my parents with full-time jobs.

When I was fourteen, I started a light and sound equipment rental company and was on the road most weekends through my high school years. After two years of military service, I returned to that business, working concerts and trade shows and other events, eventually branching out into event marketing and planning.

Mirka and I met in the month before my brother's wedding, where I was his best man and she was the maid of honor. As a professional event planner, I consulted closely with Mirka on the arrangements, although that was mostly over the phone since she was in Thailand much of that time. Soon after we finally met in person, I proposed. We married six months later.

I had thought that I had seen the big world as I toured Germany, but here was a woman who had lived on virtually every continent. Mirka was the daughter of a university professor who was highly acclaimed for his work in water technology. She was working on her doctorate in international management, and I hadn't started college.

Nonetheless, she told me that I was different from all the men with advanced degrees and big ambitions who had wanted to date her. A few had even told her that if they were to marry and have children, they would compare incomes to see which spouse would go to work and which one would stay home. Mirka wanted a partner who did not aspire to compete with her. She saw me as an intellectual equal who wasn't out to prove himself a superior scholar and wage earner.

Soon after becoming husband and wife, we also became father and mother. I became our little boy's primary caregiver while Mirka continued to pursue her career. Inspired by my father-in-law, I enrolled in civil engineering classes, with an emphasis on environmental issues, in Munich. I was just a few credits short of my bachelor's degree when Mirka's had the opportunity to advance her career by moving to the United States. Soon we were headed for Pittsburgh, Pennsylvania.

After that, our next stops were in Colorado and Michigan and back to Pittsburgh as we followed Mirka's career from one professional advancement to another. Those moves were not optional, but we saw them as opportunities, not annoyances. Her career advances were our priority.

When our son was four years old, our daughter was born, and I became the caregiver for two little ones. My responsibility was running the household, and it was a full-time job, twenty-four hours a day. There wouldn't be the time or money for me to return to college.

I did keep busy outside the house, however. I found time during those years to volunteer as a firefighter, where I taught rope rescue, and at an animal shelter as a dog trainer. For a while I also operated a handyman business, and when our son was learning to swim, I decided to become a swim official.

During those years, I also began my venture as a coach and consultant, and when my children were old enough, I found the time to write this book.

SACRIFICE AND RESPECT

"You have an amazing way of reinventing yourself each time," my wife has told me, and I know what she means. I have adjusted and adapted and found new interests, new skills, and new ways to use old skills. I did it for us, and I did it for myself.

Besides being my children's primary caretaker, I have found fulfillment in a variety of roles. I like to get my hands dirty. I like tools and woodworking. I have a collection of barbecue grills, nine in all. Some might call that guy stuff, and they might think of child care as women's stuff. It's neither. Although I am, in the eyes of many, a typical Mr. Mom, I have a unique set of interests and abilities and strengths that define me.

A MAN CAN BE SUPPORTIVE OF HIS PARTNER WITHOUT DEVOTING HIMSELF SOLELY TO THE HOUSE AND KIDS.

While some men manage the household full-time, others support their partner by scaling back their own job. Some maintain their own careers while sharing family responsibilities. A man can be supportive of his partner without devoting himself solely to the house and kids. As long as he is not an obstacle to her, and as long as he does what he can to give her the freedom to focus on her career, he is stepping up to the challenge.

The challenge is, quite simply, for the man to reinvent himself without losing himself. His goal should be to support his partner so that she can develop herself and support the family. His goal also should be to develop himself, maintaining his own interests in life and working toward a prosperous future.

Such a man is willing to sacrifice to support the woman's career, but in sacrificing, he should not abandon his own aspirations. A man who continues to work outside the home often chooses a job with flexible hours. Or he finds a job that allows him to work from home—not just any job, though. His work often will be related to a profession that he expects to develop further one day.

In other words, he continues to develop his own interests even while stepping back for a time to give priority to hers. He will continue to be himself. In a mutually supportive relationship, she will respect him for that. She will encourage his individual initiative and do what she can to help him succeed.

A GOOD START

As women rise in leadership, they continue to face the pervasive issues of gender equality and harassment that have held them back for generations. In recent years, various societal micromovements have received increasing publicity as they demand respectful and fair treatment for women. It is not just about the woman, however, because whatever limits her ability to thrive in the workplace will also limit her family and partnership. We all have a major stake in equality.

Even though women make up nearly half the work force and are getting more college degrees than men, they still earn less. According to the Institute for Women's Policy Research, full-time female employees in the United States made only 80.5 cents for every dollar that men earned for the same work in 2017.[6] That's a 20 percent wage gap. The trend is similar in other countries, and the gap exists

---

6   Institute for Women's Policy Research, "Pay Equity and Discrimination," https://iwpr.org/issue/employment-education-economic-change/pay-equity-discrimination/.

in nearly every occupation for which data exists to measure it.

The institute reported that outright discrimination persists in hiring practices, pay, and promotions. At the current slow pace of annual improvement, according to the report, it will take forty years for women to reach overall pay parity with men. For African American women, it will take a century; for Hispanic women, two centuries. Nonetheless, an NBC-*Wall Street Journal* poll in 2018 found that only one in seven men see a significant problem, but one in three women see it, and 44 percent say they personally have experienced it.[7]

Many women have felt that discrimination in the workplace worsens when they give birth, or even when a woman marries or gets engaged. The assumption is that she will be less committed to her career, and therefore she gets fewer opportunities to advance. And fathers, too, feel the effects of parenthood on their careers. Their prospects for promotion can suffer if they need to arrange their work schedule around their family obligations or take time off for family reasons. As are the women, they, too, are perceived to be more committed to their family than to their job.

Because change takes time, we must accelerate this conversation on workplace equality and the changing roles of men and women. Starting today, even if all new hires were women, it would take many years to establish equal representation on workplace executive teams. A friend recently told me about changes in the automotive industry, and his comments reminded me about the pace of change for women in the workplace. By 2025, the auto industry expects that nearly a third of all new cars produced will be electric-powered,

---

7   Carrie Dann, "Poll: Workplace Equality Stalls for Women
     Even as Perceptions Improve," NBC News, March 22,
     2018, https://www.nbcnews.com/politics/first-read/
     poll-workplace-equality-stalls-women-even-perceptions-improve-n859206

but that doesn't mean a third of the cars on a typical parking lot will be electric. It will be many years before the proportion is even 5 percent. All those internal combustion vehicles—the ones already on the road, and the new ones still being made—will keep going for a long time before they are retired from service. All those men in the workplace will keep going a long time, as well.

That illustrates why we need to get started now on promoting workplace equality. Let's take a look at a few examples of efforts to promote change:

GENDER EQUALITY. A striking example of the many projects designed to spread awareness is *Purl*, a 2019 animated short film produced by Pixar Animation Studios. The critically acclaimed film features an eager ball of pink yarn named Purl who gets a job at an investment company called BRO, where she struggles to fit in with the all-male staff of humans who disdain her presence. So, she knits herself into one of the boys and changes her personality to win their acceptance. Then she realizes she is losing her integrity and setting a poor example for all the other pink balls of yarn who might wish to follow in her path.

FIGHTING STEREOTYPES. Since when did it become an insult to say someone does something like a girl? In phrases such as *run like a girl, throw like a girl, fight like a girl* or many others, the message is that girls don't perform as well as boys. Although most people realize how such suggestions of inferiority can stifle a girl's confidence, the language persists. Various initiatives have called attention to this issue. One was a Nike commercial in the company's Dream Crazy campaign that focused on other language designed to put women down: If they show strong emotion, they're *dramatic*. If they have big dreams, they're *delusional*. If they get angry, they're *hysterical*, or *irrational*—or *crazy*. After highlighting women's accomplishments in athletics, the narrator states, "So if they want to call you crazy, show them what crazy is."

SOCIAL MOVEMENTS. After sexual abuse allegations were publicized against film producer Harvey Weinstein in 2017, dozens of women came forward with additional claims against him. Soon, women were stepping forward in what became known as the Weinstein effect to accuse powerful men around the world. The wave of allegations built into two prominent social movements, MeToo and Time's Up, accelerated by the power of the social media.

The MeToo movement spread virally after the well-publicized Weinstein allegations. As prominent women added their voices, MeToo encouraged women who had been abused and harassed by men, particularly in the workplace, to speak out. As the movement built in 2018, Hollywood celebrities founded Time's Up, which raised a multimillion dollar legal defense fund to battle sexual harassment and rallied hundreds of volunteer attorneys. These movements brought widespread attention to the prevalence of abuse against women in our society. Many men also have added their voices to the cause, proclaiming that such behavior must not be tolerated. These movements are not antimale. They are antiwrongdoing.

CORPORATE EFFORTS. "We Believe," a 2019 commercial by Gillette, is a prime example of how companies can step up and challenge us all to get to the heart of pervasive issues in our society. Focusing on issues of bullying, sexism, sexual harassment, and male chauvinism, the commercial was part of the company's three-year commitment to donate to organizations helping men to "achieve their personal best." Though some people criticized the commercial as sexist itself for taking a dim view of men, the message seemed clear enough: men should be respectful, stand up and speak out, show empathy, and serve as good examples for the next generation. It's hard to argue with that.

All those efforts are a good start, and the issues deserve the attention and recognition they are getting. But they also have elicited negative responses as well as positive, which shows that our society has a long way to go to ensuring fair treatment for women.

I recently met artist and musician J. G. Boccella, who has become a champion for the advancement of women in the workplace. Many of his portraits are of powerful women whom he has met. He captured their strength on canvas and resolved to take the next step by founding FierceWomenProject.com and authoring *The Official FierceWomen VISIONBOOK*, which uses portrait art as a platform for women leaders to share their stories and inspire the next generation. He is also a keynote speaker, and the author of *Bring Your Strength*, an invitation for men to cocreate and colead with women.

A few men will never accept a world that gives women an equal footing, Boccella says. They are hostile to the idea of diversity. Others simply do not recognize any problem. They see no need for change. Our best hope, he says, lies in the gray area between the activists and the deniers: the men most open to new ways of thinking. They are the hidden demographic that we can reach.

> OUR BEST HOPE LIES IN THE GRAY AREA BETWEEN THE ACTIVISTS AND THE DENIERS: THE MEN MOST OPEN TO NEW WAYS OF THINKING.

Once they become aware, these men may very likely be willing to step forward and take a different approach in their partnerships.

CHAPTER 9

AS SOCIETY SLOWLY AWAKES

SOCIETY PILLAR

As men and women strive to create mutually supportive partnerships, they must deal with a tide of public perception that is slow to change. Old attitudes fade slowly, as many still believe that each sex should keep its place. Nothing is wrong with a traditional arrangement if it works well for each of the partners and for the family. In countless families, however, that place is changing. In time, the attitudes will change too.

*This chapter showcases **the society pillar:** how far society has come, and how far society must still go.*

The school secretary had been trying to reach Mirka for an hour or two, unaware that she was on a flight to Europe. Viktoria had gone down the slide during recess, not realizing that it was wet from rain. Her pants were soaked through. Over and over, the secretary called Mirka's number, to no avail. She left several messages.

Meanwhile, I was at home, five minutes away. Nobody asked Viktoria which parent was in charge of looking out for her interests during school hours. And Viktoria did not think to ask the nurse to call her dad. Even though the school had my contact information, the presumption was that this was a job for a mom. Finally, I did get a call, and I was off to the school in a flash with a change of clothes for her.

I can see how such situations happen, but understanding them doesn't excuse them. I could have been there in a few minutes so that Viktoria could get back to her classroom.

Our society has a long way to go in dispelling old assumptions about who will be responsible for doing what in a family. On many school forms, for example, there is no checkbox to indicate which parent should be called first. The mother's name is requested first, with the father as the backup. Federal tax forms list the man's name first when a couple files jointly, and they are filed under his Social Security number in the assumption that he is the head of household and responsible for the family's finances. How hard could it be to make such forms gender neutral? It would be far easier for everyone involved. Gay parents, for example, would not have to decide who was going to be the dad and who was going to be the mom. On the forms, they simply could be Parent No. 1 and Parent No. 2. What matters is that the appropriate person, regardless of anatomy, be available for the children when they need help.

Those school and tax form policies are just a couple of specific examples of how slowly society wakes up to the realities of our changing family cultures. Change tends to begin not in the big arenas but in the small places. Innovation is often started by individual entrepreneurs, not corporations that are ever alert to stakeholder risk. And change starts within the family unit long before governments and institutions recognize what is happening.

CHANGE TENDS TO BEGIN NOT IN THE BIG ARENAS BUT IN THE SMALL PLACES.

In countless families today, both partners work outside the home, sometimes just to pay the bills but often to pursue their career ambitions. In many other families, men are filling the support role at home while women excel in the workplace. In 2017, according to the Center for American Progress, 41 percent of mothers were either the sole breadwinner for their families or earned more than half the total household income.[8] That figure includes single working mothers and married mothers who out-earn their husbands. Still, most of society tends to carry on as usual, as if oblivious to the deep social currents that are changing our world. It takes time to overcome the status quo.

Eventually, society does catch up and adjust to new realities, but that lag frustrates progress. In this age of technology, for example, the majority of people in the United States still uses paper checks, whereas in China, most transactions are conducted via mobile phones. And bureaucrats still seem to prefer paper forms when people should be able to easily upload information online. Governments are only beginning to accept what others have been doing for many years now. For many institutions throughout the world, adapting to technology and trends is a long and slow process.

---

8   Sarah Jane Glynn, Center for American Progress, May 10, 2019, "Breadwinning mothers Continue to Be the US Norm," https://www.americanprogress.org/issues/women/reports/2019/05/10/469739/breadwinning-mothers-continue-u-s-norm/.

EVOLUTION
OF ATTITUDES

Engrained attitudes also take years to evolve into acceptance. The tide of public opinion can slow progress to a crawl. When men do step forward in the family support role so women can focus on their careers, their friends seem quick to offer their opinions on the matter. On one level, their comments might seem like good-natured teasing, but in truth, they cut. "Oh, I see you got the better deal here, sleeping late and playing golf and drinking beer all day," they say, as if taking care of the kids allowed much time for any of that. I doubt that most of them would say such things to a woman who takes care of her kids. But they feel free to say it to a man, and the insinuation is this: "Oh, I see you're doing women's work. You should get a real job and be a real man." To make matters worse, he may be saying something like that to himself.

It's not solely the men who carry such attitudes, though. Some women feel uneasy about men filling the homemaker role, as if that were a trespass on their territory. These may be women at the pinnacle of success, yet they hesitate to hand over a responsibility that they still feel deep inside defines their womanhood. Nor will some women consider hiring a man for child care, and not just because they think only women possess the nurturing skills to do it right. (Let's face it. Changing diapers isn't a genetically imprinted skill.) Their attitude seems more of a protective stance, because, well, you never know.

Successful women often feel the judgment of other women, as well. It's not their imagination: Full-time moms sometimes signal their disdain, subtly or not, for the career woman, whom they consider to be a part-time mom, or no kind of mom at all. They may imply that she is a bad wife, too, as if to say, "If you loved your husband, you wouldn't expect him to be taking care of your kids. Why would you do this to him?" And to make matters worse, she may be saying something like that to herself.

Women send women the same sort of message that men send men: "You should keep your place!" Whether you are a man or a woman, understand that you are not alone if you feel frustrated by that attitude. Nor are you alone if you feel ambivalent about your role in the family. Your parents probably maintained the traditional roles, and to some extent that shaped your expectations. That doesn't mean you aren't doing the right thing now for yourself. Taking your own path shows no disrespect for your parents. By understanding the root of your feelings, you can rise above your own inner stereotypes to proudly try something new.

Sometimes, upon learning of my role in our family, men view me as a curiosity and feel compelled to point out that their job is to venture out into the big world to make the big bucks. I could do that, but I know it would take quite some time to earn what Mirka can make now. Making the big bucks is her job. My job is to make sure that she gets the support she needs to continue doing it well.

And that's the job that more and more men are proudly accepting. For generations, women have supported men so that they can thrive in their careers. As the old saying goes, "Behind every great man is a great woman." It's time for an update: "At the side of every great woman is a great man." Mirka knows that she needs me as much as I know that I need her. Together we can do a great job of raising a family, fulfilling our dreams, reaching our goals, and advancing in life. Yes, each of us still deals with inner conflicts.

IT'S TIME FOR AN UPDATE: "AT THE SIDE OF EVERY GREAT WOMAN IS A GREAT MAN."

Each of us has felt the sting of lingering societal attitudes that seek to drive us down, but we choose to rise up. We support each other. That is the beauty of a harmonious partnership.

CHANGE IN SMALL PLACES

Often, when companies and organizations sponsor events such as dinners or parties for employees or members, they also arrange outings or buy gifts for the spouses who will be attending. I have been to many such events as the accompanying spouse. The outing sometimes has been a destination to shop for women's apparel. That's not something that ordinarily is top my list of things to do. And I have received gifts such as handbags, jewelry, and flowers. Our daughter seems to appreciate them when I pass them on to her.

I met a man who accompanied his wife to her company's holiday party, where the organizers had arranged team-building exercises for both the employees and their spouses. He was expected to join a group of women making wreathes. Those gestures were meant to be thoughtful, but with just a little more thought, the results could have been far more meaningful. Even if the organizer of such an event knows that most of the spouses will be women, that organizer could still provide gifts and activities that would be appreciated by virtually anyone.

A bottle of wine is fine, for example, unless it's an Alcoholics Anonymous gathering, in which case it would be inappropriate, just as a rose is inappropriate for a man who would prefer a wrench. Kitchen goods, such as a nice set of cutlery, can be appreciated by whoever is responsible for the household, whether a man or a woman. A technical gadget could suitable for either sex.

Whenever Mirka has organized events for her company's employees and their spouses, she has been careful to see that the activities and gifts are appropriate to either sex or are gender neutral. I, too, keep that in mind as I plan events for the YPO. I have arranged some specifically for the male spouses of female executives, but my preference is to work on gender-neutral events. I like to emphasize the importance of the role itself, not the sex of the person fulfilling it.

Years ago, as an event planner in Germany, I made my share of mistakes. I arranged for gifts such as flowers, or visits to a spa, without thinking much about whether the recipients would be men or women. Today, because of my role in my own household, I have become more sensitive to the significance not only of the big picture but also of the little things, the ones that might seem almost insignificant but can have a big impact. Change, after all, starts in small places.

Society needs such sensitivity. We need to become more gender neutral. Far better to think in broad terms of interests. We would all benefit if society were to pay more attention to the needs and dignity of people regardless of sex. We would be better off focusing on who does what, rather than on who we believe should be doing what. That sensitivity would resolve many of the issues that we have been discussing in this chapter.

Even though society is getting used to strong women in the workplace, men who take care of the house and kids are still often seen as an oddity. Their contributions still go largely unrecognized outside the family. Our society has a long way to go toward fair treatment of women, but the conversation at least has started. We have scarcely begun considering the other side, however. What about the partners at home? What about all those men who, in one way or another, are supporting women's progress? That conversation needs to be opened up, as well.

The five pillars that we have examined in this book are the infrastructure supporting the rise of women leaders. They do more, though; they also hold up the men who are the women's partners in life, and the children of those couples, and the generations to come. That's a heavy responsibility.

One of those pillars is society itself, which has been slow to adapt to the quickening pace of change. We must strengthen that pillar. As more couples consider nontraditional partnerships, they will need the counsel of those who have gone before them and the tools to help them succeed. Their children need to witness good role models—men as well as women—who demonstrate that they will not be limited by other people's expectations. Girls and boys need to see women who "lean in" to their careers, as Sheryl Sandberg puts it, and men who are willing to give those women someone to lean on.

Male role models are out there, in greater numbers every day, waiting to step out of the shadows. They, too, face daily struggles as they adapt to a new way of living. Mirka has told me that my adjustment to a nontraditional family role has probably been more difficult than her adjustment in the workplace. She finds more acceptance as a female executive than I find as a male homemaker—and that's saying a lot, since women have long been facing a great many obstacles in the workplace.

It's time for change, all around, as men and women step forward together into a brighter future, supporting each other for the greater good. Let's do this right. Our families and future generations are depending on us.

TRY, FAIL, TRY AGAIN

The chandelier was 150 years old, my son told me, and so valuable that nobody was allowed to touch it. "They have to wear gloves even to polish it," he said. Dominik was recounting the highlights of his third-grade field trip to the capitol building in Lansing, Michigan.

I smiled and gestured toward the shelf behind him in our living room, where Mirka displayed a collection of her family's Czech crystal. "Now you see why Mom and Dad always yell when you guys toss your jacket over there or bounce a ball in the room!"

My grandmother's house in Germany was built in the twelfth century. By Old World standards, this isn't particularly unusual, but it is ancient by the standards of many people in America, a vast land of ever-changing landscapes that my family has been privileged to explore. European settlers crossed the ocean for a fresh start in a new world, hoping to expand their horizons and improve their living conditions in whatever way they wanted to.

In all our worlds, we must keep alive that spirit of hope and initiative. We must respect the old ways and appreciate the beauty of traditions that have stood the test of time. They are like fine crystal, and we must not carelessly break them.

In these chapters, we have explored ways to accommodate the needs of today's partnerships. We have examined the five pillars of support for women as they rise to their rightful place as business leaders. We cannot afford to squander that talent.

We have also offered a vision of a society in which men celebrate gender equality in meaningful ways. Successful men have long leaned on women for support. In the new world of partnerships, successful women, increasingly, are leaning on supportive men. Loved ones can bring out the best in each other by understanding and accepting each other's strengths and weaknesses, living and working in harmony. They can take on unaccustomed roles and handle them exceedingly well.

To accomplish anything, however, you must get started. Though you may be unsure of those first steps, seek out good advice and take an educated guess on what will work out best. Along the way, you may fail, but that suggests only one thing: You have learned something. You are growing. You and your family are evolving in your own unique way. Try again, adjust course as necessary, and expect to succeed.